Shiny Objects Marketing

Shiny Objects Marketing

Using Simple Human Instincts to
Make Your Brand Irresistible

DAVID A. LaBONTE

WILEY

John Wiley & Sons, Inc.

Published by John Wiley & Sons, Inc., Hoboken, New Jersey.
Published simultaneously in Canada.

For general information on our other products and services or for technical support, please contact our Customer Care Department within the United States at (800) 762-2974, outside the United States at (317) 572-3993 or fax (317) 572-4002.

Wiley also publishes its books in a variety of electronic formats. Some content that appears in print may not be available in electronic books. For more information about Wiley products, visit our web site at www.wiley.com.

Library of Congress Cataloging-in-Publication Data
LaBonte, David A., 1953-
    Shiny objects marketing : using simple human instincts to make your brand irresistible / David A. LaBonte.
       p.   cm.
    Includes bibliographical references and index.
    ISBN 978-0-470-35767-5 (cloth)
       1.   Marketing—Psychological aspects.   2.   Product management.   I. Title.
HF5415.L23 2009
658.8'343—dc22

                                                                 2008020130

Printed in the United States of America.

10   9   8   7   6   5   4   3   2   1

To Rosemary—my muse, my soul mate, and my shiny object

Contents

About the Author

As a senior strategic executive with over 30 years marketing and advertising experience, David A. LaBonte has worked on accounts for such famous brands as Fantastic Sams, Subway Sandwiches, Intel, Mitsubishi, Texas Instruments, MADD, GE/Sanyo, Crystal Geyser, and Motorola. His unique background of working for manufacturers, distributors, and advertising agencies provides him with a powerful insight across all marketing functions.

The concept of Shiny Objects Marketing came to the author over a decade ago while attending an endless marketing seminar. In the midst of the boredom, his brain began to shout, "Come on! It's simpler than that! Make your brand a shiny object, and you'll sell truckloads." Since that time, he has successfully implemented the Shiny Object Marketing concept with a wide variety of industries and clients.

Mr. LaBonte is president and partner of AdMatrix, an Orange County, California-based marketing/advertising agency with clients across the country. His agency has become a destination for companies seeking a way to discover their customers' shiny objects. Mr. LaBonte conducts Shiny Objects Marketing Workshops to help companies of all sizes implement the powerful concept presented in this book. For additional information on these workshops, visit www.admatrix.net.

Preface: What's the Big Deal?

Sometimes the simplest concepts are the hardest to see, but have the greatest impact on life. And so it is with Shiny Objects Marketing.

One of two things usually happens when I explain the concept of Shiny Objects Marketing to people. They either give me a dumbfounded look and say, "Yeah, so?" as though they've known this principle all their lives and are wondering what the big deal is; or they let the thought bounce around in their heads for a few moments, congealing and gathering momentum and then suddenly light up as though they've just undergone a spiritual awakening. The latter "gets it." The former has a lot of work to do to scrape away the obviousness from the glasses through which they view life. They are the same people who look at a sunset and simply see the sun going down, while the latter group sees a beautiful masterpiece of creation. The more you're willing to give in to the notion of Shiny Objects Marketing, the more you will see fundamental and life-changing applications that this concept can bring to your everyday world.

For the reader who is involved with, or responsible for, moving products out the door, the simple fact is that once you understand the power and influence of shiny objects, your marketing will be altered forever. You will never look at your customers the same way, and you will never approach advertising the same way, ever again.

You won't be able to go back. It's like one of those pictures with two drawings intertwined into one. Usually you can only see one of the drawings until someone points out the other. After that, even if you try, you can't help but see both drawings. Your perception has been irrevocably expanded.

For the nonmarketing person (which is most of the world), Shiny Objects Marketing will help you see human relationships in a whole new light. You'll understand it isn't your shiny object that motivates others; it's their shiny object. In other words, people don't always see things from your perspective. To assume that your shiny object is the same as theirs is to assume that they share all your life experiences and view the world exactly as you do. This is simply not the case. Individuals have their own set of needs and concerns that create their unique set of shiny objects. If you want to relate to people, you need to discover what their shiny objects are.

This book is the result of banging my head against the marketing wall for over 30 years. I've worked in advertising and marketing for my entire professional life. I've heard every theory and complex analogy conceivable. The concept of Shiny Objects Marketing came to me while attending another endless marketing seminar where the speaker was droning on and on about something having to do with making sure your click-through rate has a direct corollary to your recent frequency monetary value ratio while maintaining advertising elasticity. I remember my brain shouting, "Come on! It's got to be simpler than that!"

And it is.

So, here's the big concept. Are you ready?

After all these years—after all the dissertations and highbrow seminars, after all the deep reaching psychological profiling—it simply comes down to this:

> People, as all creatures, are innately attracted to shiny objects. If you can make your brand, product, or service a shiny object to your customers and prospects, you'll be immensely successful.

There it is. That's what you shelled out the money for.

At this point, some of you will say, "Yeah, so? What's the big deal?" The rest of you are feeling those thoughts beginning to bounce around.

To that second group, let's get started.

1 | What Can You Expect from This Book?

To a large extent, that's up to you.

Although Shiny Objects Marketing is an extremely simple principle, catching a glimpse of its full meaning and putting it into practice can often prove difficult. This book helps people find their customers' shiny objects. To accomplish this, we will go through a step-by-step approach that will help you answer the following:

1. What are the origins of shiny objects?
2. What will stop your customers in their tracks and make them notice your product?
3. What will make them want to take a closer look?
4. How do you get them to reach out, touch your product, and try it?
5. What emotions are created when someone experiences your product?
6. What will make them want to grab your product and not let go?

For thousands of years, people have gazed upward, fascinated by the shiny objects in the sky. We have an innate attraction to shiny objects all around us. They catch our eye. We place great value on them. We wear them to attract attention to ourselves. We even worship them. Some cultures believe they hold the very essence of life. They relate to our primal nature and are the base of the instincts we share with all creatures. Ultimately, we reach for the brass ring because it is shiny.

The principles taught in this book are not just about selling the next corkscrew or hair clip. They're about creating brands that can't be ignored. While other marketing concepts use meaningless buzzwords, worn-out clichés, and impossible-to-replicate programs, Shiny Objects Marketing relates to almost any person, regardless of marketing experience or budget. It reaches right down to our primeval instincts and taps into forces we can't resist.

3

Shiny Object's Evil Twin

Before we get too deeply involved in this discussion, I need to point out a huge misunderstanding in the world at large. Most people understand shiny objects to be anything that distracts them from their primary focus. A shiny object by this definition for the college student studying for a test is an invitation to go to a party. For the programmer who must complete a given assignment by the end of the week, it is a hot, new video game that just came out. For the politician who strays from his primary pledge, it is an attractive special interest initiative. These are all examples of the dark side of shiny objects. They are the negative mirror image of positive shiny objects.

Curiously enough, if you Google the phrase "shiny object," almost all of the references you find will be for this evil twin interpretations. However, if we are innately attracted to something, isn't it in our best interest to understand why? If we simply try to ignore our own impulses, those impulses begin to feed on our subconscious. Conversely, if we try to understand why we are drawn to a shiny object, we can learn something more about both the shiny object and ourselves. We can understand the nature of the attraction. Then we can choose whether or not to follow that shiny object. If we decide that the shiny object would have a negative impact on our lives, then at the very least, we have a better idea of how to counteract its attraction.

Shiny Objects Marketing is an entirely new way to look at shiny objects. Most of us have been conditioned to believe that shiny objects are bad because they draw us away from our primary purpose. Shiny objects, in general, are maligned as casual distractions from our main objectives in life. But what if those shiny objects *are* our main objectives in life? As we will discuss later in this book, the shiny objects that are the most powerful are those with deep, intrinsic value. Family, prosperity, security, and happiness—these are all worthy goals in life, and they are all shiny objects, as well.

I invite you to put aside any negative associations you may have with shiny objects. Despite the frequent warnings of those around you who might say, "Keep your attention focused on the goal and don't pay any attention to shiny objects," we're going to show you how valuable and productive it can be to focus on the shiny objects. The basic approach of Shiny Objects Marketing is to accept the natural attraction of shiny objects as a universal truth and suggest methods to put that attraction to work in positive ways. In other words, don't fight it—use it.

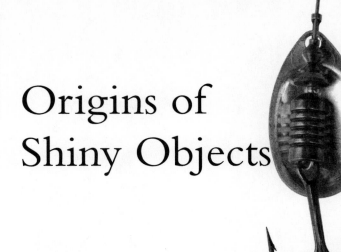

2

Origins of Shiny Objects

Since the beginning of time, almost all creatures, including humans, have had an innate attraction to bright, shiny objects. This impulse is overwhelming and often impossible to suppress. For thousands of generations, mankind has gazed at the night sky, fascinated by the billions of pinholes of light. Magnificent stories and legends have been written about the stars. Entire populations have based their religious beliefs on and tracked their future by the arrangement and movement of these heavenly shiny objects.

As a young boy, I went on numerous campouts into the Sierra Nevada Mountains. The air was so pure and clean that the brilliance of the stars was magnified a hundred times. I could not resist the temptation to sleep out under the stars. I would lie in my sleeping bag in the middle of a meadow in the cool night air, staring up into this infinite spectacle, mesmerized by the wonder of it all. Like millions before me, I had an innate attraction to these tiny spots of light—these shiny objects that I could scarcely comprehend.

One animal most known for its irresistible urge to grab shiny objects is the raccoon. In the classic children's book *Where the Red Fern Grows*, author Wilson Rawls (1961) writes about how to trap a raccoon. He explains that you first drill a small hole in a log. Next, you hammer some nails into the log around the hole so that they stick out into the hole at an angle. Finally, you drop something shiny, like a coin, into the hole in the log. The raccoon, once discovering the shiny object cannot contain its curiosity and reaches into the hole to grab it. Once the raccoon wraps its paw around the object, the paw becomes too big to come out of the hole, and the nails trap the raccoon. All the raccoon needs to do to set itself free is let go of the shiny object. However, the desire to possess the shiny object is stronger than the desire to be free; so the raccoon will clutch the object for days. Even when the hunter returns, the raccoon would rather die than give up the shiny object.

To use another example from the animal kingdom, the common phrase "like a deer in the headlights" strongly illustrates this point.

The deer that suddenly is faced with an oncoming car is so awe-struck by the bright shiny headlights, that, rather than run for cover, it becomes frozen in its tracks. The unfortunate driver who thinks the deer will eventually come to its senses and scamper away is usually left to deal with a smashed front end and a pitiful, dead creature.

Birds—especially magpies—are renowned for being attracted to shiny objects. The female magpie uses this primeval instinct to her advantage. To attract a mate, she weaves bits of wire, aluminum foil, or other shiny objects into her nest. When the male magpie flies by, he becomes completely smitten by the bling. He simply can't resist. So strong is this attraction that magpies often become mates for life—all in all, not too terribly different from humans.

Fishermen also know the value of a good shiny object. Every summer while growing up, I went trout fishing with my father. My favorite lure was called the Super Duper. The name, as I came to realize many years later, was a double entendre, in that it "duped" fish into chasing it. It was a very simple lure consisting of a piece of shiny metal bent into a narrow U shape. The current of the stream caused it to spin, creating a wonderful shimmering effect. When all else failed, I would pull out my Super Duper, and the fish had no defense. They could not escape the magnetic pull of this shiny object.

People are no different from the rest of the animal kingdom when it comes to shiny objects. Our primitive instincts attract us to bright, shiny objects innately. Sometimes the appeal—greed or lust—for the object is so strong that some people will grasp it with clenched fists, even to their own detriment. Alternatively, there are a great many *positive* shiny objects that we are attracted to, like family and friends. The attractions of these shiny objects are equally strong and have often compelled people to make great sacrifices just to hold on to them.

Shiny objects can be good or evil—and both types have the ability to capture our attention. Whichever type we reach for is up to us. Although we often can't help looking at shiny objects, we have the final vote regarding the ones we end up possessing.

From Objects of Desire to Objects of Worship

Shiny objects often carry far greater meaning than just being attractive baubles. In fact, over the millennia, mankind has elevated these glimmering items to godhood.

For instance, the Chinese began to make jade objects 7,000 years ago during the New Stone Age. When drawn from the earth, jade looks fairly plain and dull. Because of its durability, it was used for axe heads, knives, and other weapons. However, along the way, some intelligent soul discovered that you could polish jade into a brilliant luster. Suddenly, what used to be just a hard rock was now a shiny object and an item of attraction and desire. So much so that jade quickly became a primary form of currency. The craving for jade actually became so great that sometime between 3400–2250 bc the Liangzhu culture in the Ningshao area of the Yangtze River Delta completely depleted one of the richest deposits of jade in the world (Liu 2003).

Once its brilliant, shiny nature had been uncovered, it didn't take long for jade to make its way into spiritual customs. According to Li Liu, jade was used to create ceremonial objects, ranging from religious decorative items to jade burial suits. In the *Book of the Later Han* (n.d.), one of the official Chinese historical works that was compiled by Fan Ye in the fifth century, the materials and manner of construction of these suits depended on the person's social stature, but only the wealthiest of aristocrats could afford one. The Chinese believed jade had magical properties and could preserve the body. To this day, heaven is depicted in the person of the Emperor of Heaven or the Jade Emperor in popular Chinese religion. It is interesting that of all the titles that could have been conferred on the supreme being, the name of a shiny object was chosen.

Since the earliest origins of religion or the belief in deities, shiny objects have been used by the faithful to demonstrate their piety and devotion. These shiny objects have acted as an inexplicable link between mankind and the great beyond. Some sociologists have theorized that this connection stems from a primal attraction to glistening water, the basic necessity for survival. Others agree that this affinity for shiny objects does relate to water, but suggest that it dates back to when humans first sloshed forth from the primeval ocean and sprouted legs. The water was our collective womb and, as a result, our common origin or creator. No matter what theory is correct, it is clear that almost every ancient and many modern religions see shiny objects as a way to connect with the universe.

In 1532, when the Spaniards invaded Peru, they devastated the culture and literally wiped out an entire religion that had existed for centuries. Almost every trace of the religion was destroyed. What we do know about this ancient Incan religion is that it was steeped in ritual and symbolism. These icons were engraved on and depicted in countless works of gold and silver. Incas called gold the "sweat of the sun"; the most sacred of all deities. Every ounce of gold and silver artifacts, except for a few precious remnants, was melted down and taken back to Spain as plunder. According to an article in the *International Herald Tribune*, well-known international art scholar Souren Melikian (2001) calculates the Spaniards melted down more than 633 tons of silver and 190 tons of gold.

In her book *Rain of the Moon: Silver in Ancient Peru*, Heidi King (2000, 15) relates the story of a Spanish soldier, Pedro the Cieza de Leon, who made an account of what he saw in one of the temples in 1547. He wrote that he gazed at

> an image of the sun, of great size, made of gold, beautifully wrought and set with many precious stones. . . . There was a garden in which the earth was lumps of fine gold and it was cunningly planted with stalks of corn that were of gold—stalk, leaves, and ears. . . . Aside from this, there were more than 20 sheep of gold with their lambs, and the shepherds who guarded them with their slings and staffs, all of this metal. There were many tubs of gold and silver and emeralds, and goblets, pots, and every kind of vessel all of fine gold.

In short, it was one of the richest temples in the entire world.

The few relics that survived make it clear that the ancient Incas believed in a firm association between shiny objects and the after-life. In fact, these shiny objects seemed requisite to gain immortality, according to Melikian (2001):

> Recent excavations at Sipan [a large religious center in Peru] have uncovered tombs in which gold objects were consistently placed on the right side of the deceased and silver on the left. Scholars relate this to early Spanish reports that the Indians associated gold with the right side and silver with the left, and also with masculinity and femininity. But it is enough to suggest that symbolism, not just aesthetics, dictated the combination of gold and silver.

Even in Buddhism, a religion that traditionally shuns material-ism, shiny objects play a major role. Most Tibetan Buddhist ritual implements and sacrificial objects were cast in gold, silver, or copper. Statues of Buddha are commonly made from gold and other pre-cious metals and stones. The most dramatic of these is located in Mandalay, the capital of old Myanmar (formerly Burma). In an ancient temple with a terraced roof of gilt stucco and walls that were once decorated with elaborate frescos there resides one of largest religious effigies in the world. It is called Maha Muni, and it is the largest golden Buddha in the world, topping over 15 feet in height and entirely gilded in a two-inch layer of gold. It is estimated that it is encrusted with nearly two tons of gold. The gold crown and the body ornaments of the statue are solid gold with hundreds of precious gems including rubies, sapphires, emeralds, jade, dia-monds, and pearls—all of which were donated by pious devotees.

Although it is pervasive, not all adoration of shiny objects has been viewed as acceptable by certain cultures. In Jewish and Christian belief, the Israelites committed a grievous sin by turning to the gods of Egypt and creating a golden calf with which to wor-ship God. It is interesting to note that the Apis Bull, the Egyptian god whom the Israelites imitated, was rarely made from gold. It was usually carved from stone. However, according to the Old Testament, while Moses was away at Mount Sinai to receive the Ten Commandments, the people began to become impatient and demanded that Aaron, Moses' brother-in-law and chief high priest, build a god whom they could worship. Evidentially, to ratchet up the event, he commanded them to "break off the golden earrings, which are in the ears of your wives, of your sons, and of your daughters, and bring them unto me" (Ex 32:2, King James Version). He then melted them down and fashioned a golden idol in the form of a calf. When Moses returned, his wrath was so unbridled that he threw down the stone tablets God had given him and broke them into pieces.

Just a scant 500 years later, the Israelites returned to using shiny objects in their rituals by adorning the Temple of Solomon with gold. According to the Old Testament, in the temple's Holy of Holies (considered the dwelling place of God), the walls were lined with sculptured cedar overlaid with gold. Chains of gold further marked the inner sanctum off from the Holy of Holies. The floor of the Temple was made of fir overlaid with gold. The doorposts and the doors leading into the Holy of Holies were constructed with olive wood. On both sets of doors were carved cherubim, palm trees, and flowers, all overlaid with gold (1Kgs 6, King James Version).

A few centuries later, Christian cathedrals throughout Europe continued the shiny object tradition of the Temple of Solomon and were richly gilded from top to bottom and decorated with precious gems. Some of these houses of worship are more lavish than the most ornate palaces. Case in point: Saint Mark's Basilica in Venice is considered by many to be the most opulent cathedral in all of Europe. This church, which many believe to be the resting place of Saint Mark's remains, is decorated with gilded statues, polished marble, golden sculptures, and elaborate frescos. Over the centuries, the Venetians have embellished it with works of art and precious jewels from around the world.

The most unique feature of this building is the Byzantine mosaic illustrations that line the walls. They were crafted from millions of gold tiles and depict stories from the Bible; allegorical figures; and events in the lives of Christ, the Virgin Mary, Saint Mark, and other saints. The rays of light that sift in through the small windows that ring the base of the gilded domes strike the mosaics and create an almost blinding glitter. Houses of worship, such a Saint Mark's, stand as a testament of people's connection between God, shiny objects, and man.

The underlying motivation of such ornamentation often stems from a desire to adorn objects of worship with the most precious of possessions to demonstrate devotion. Of course, this supposes that what is precious to mankind is also precious to God. Or perhaps, it merely displays the willingness of humans to sacrifice anything that is precious to us. Either way, people have been attempting to show their devoutness by decorating their gods with shiny objects since the beginning of time. Since the attraction to shiny objects seems to be encoded in our DNA, it is reasonable to assume that it has been around as long as humans. It is definitely nothing new.

3 | Why Are We Attracted to Shiny Objects?

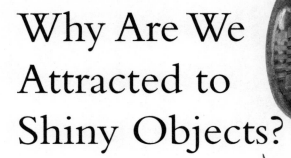

The purpose of this book is to help you make your brand a shiny object, so that people are unable to resist it. However, before you try to emulate a shiny object, it is important to understand why human beings are attracted to them in the first place. Oddly enough, even though humans and other creatures have been attracted to shiny objects since the beginning of time, there has been very little research conducted on *why*.

On one hand, mankind has always accepted this fascination as an innate phenomenon, but only in recent years have scientists and psychologists begun to probe this fundamental instinct.

On the other hand, there has been significant research into the effects of light on the human physiology and psychology. And since shiny objects reflect light—and it is really that reflection that catches our attention—it is reasonable to assume that many of the effects of light on humans have a correlation to shiny objects.

Physiological Attraction

Humans, like other creatures, evolved under sunlight. Our bodies adapted to constant exposure to sunlight, and even began to rely on it for our overall health. For this reason, many scientists believe we have a strong attraction to light built into our DNA. So, in part, our attraction to shiny objects is an extension of this physiological need. Simply put, we are attracted to light because we crave its healthful qualities.

In a 2001 report titled "Therapeutic Effects of Light in Humans," Joan E. Roberts, professor of chemistry at Fordham University, states

> Daylight, in particular visible light, is important to our overall health and well-being. Visible light not only relieves depression and circadian imbalances but also may have a positive effect on our immune responses. Although improper exposure to ultraviolet radiation can be damaging, the judicious use of ultraviolet light can be useful in treating diseases such as atopic dermatitis, lupus erythematosus, and rickets. Sunlight and

19

dark nights have been with us since the beginning of life on this planet, and as we have seen here, we have just begun to understand what powerful effects both have on human health. (p. 11)

As humans, we don't merely *enjoy* the sunshine; it is critical to our good health.

The treatment for jaundice (a disease common in infants that is caused by extremely high levels of bilirubin) was one of the earliest forms of light therapy. In 1958, a nurse in England noticed that infants exposed to sunlight did not become as jaundiced as infants who were not exposed to sunlight. This led to the first clinical use of phototherapy—using fluorescent lights to successfully treat jaundiced infants (Roberts 2001, 3).

Another positive effect of light is the boost it gives the immune system. For thousands of generations, the standard therapy for the infirm was to sit out in the sunshine. Evidently, our ancestors were smarter than we thought. When visible light hits the retina, it sends a signal to the suprachiasmatic nucleus (SCN) in the hypothalamus, and triggers the pituitary and pineal glands. The end result is an increase in cortisol, serotonin, gaba, and dopamine levels, all of which increase the strength of the immune system (Roberts 2001, 3, 7).

Our skin is an alternative pathway that light uses to boost our immune system. Laboratory studies have shown that after half an hour of exposing a small skin area to visible light, healthy subjects experienced enhanced activity of both white blood cells (which engulf and ingest foreign particles) and natural killer cells (which destroy tumor cells). Basically, light heals us from the inside (Roberts 2001, 8).

But light can heal us from the outside, as well. Visible light in the form of low level laser irradiation appears to accelerate wound healing. In clinical applications, chronic leg ulcers and Achilles tendon injuries have healed more quickly after irradiation from a laser. It appears that the light stimulates the proliferation of cells required for healing (Roberts 2001, 9).

Just as the presence of light in moderation is therapeutic to the human body, the absence of light is extremely detrimental. As mentioned previously, when sunlight enters the eye and strikes the retina, a complex reaction is set in motion in which a wide variety of glands are activated. Subsequently, this activity slows down at night and then picks up again the next day. This on-and-off switch creates an internal cycle called the circadian rhythm (Roberts 2001, 4). According to Roberts, "the oscillation of hormones it [the circadian rhythm] induces has a profound effect on most physiological functions in the body. When this process is disrupted through environmental light changes, it may lead to some of the more damaging emotional and physiological effects associated with seasonal depression (SAD), jet lag, and shift work" (Roberts 2001, 5).

Seasonal Affective Disorder (SAD) is an often-severe form of depression that occurs in regions that routinely become overcast and dark during the fall and winter months. And right on schedule, this depression dissipates in the spring. This phenomenon is highly affected by latitude. For example, only 2 percent of the population of Florida is routinely stricken with this infirmity, compared with 10 percent in New Hampshire. While it is not completely clear exactly what chemical imbalances cause this depression, the cure is quite obvious: more sunlight. It has been clinically proven that seasonal depression can be treated with light therapy that consists of the daily administration of visible light in the very early morning. Humans are so dependent on light that the effects of this type of light therapy typically produce positive results in only about three to four days (Roberts 2001, 4).

Mine workers routinely suffer from depression and other maladies as a result of light depravation. One might be inclined to say, "Well of course mine workers get depressed. Wouldn't you if you had to work all day in a hole in the ground that could crash down on top of you any minute?" An obvious observation. But there is much more to it than meets the eye (no pun intended). As described previously, the constant disruption of the circadian rhythm wreaks havoc on everything from psychological health to the immune system. People who have to work the graveyard shift often experience these kinds of problems. The effects are particularly acute among people who are constantly changing their shift hours from daytime to nighttime. The constant disruption of the circadian rhythm can result in severe psychological and physiological aliments such as sleeping difficulties, confusion and irritability, problems with metabolism, enhanced susceptibility to infectious disease and, in some extreme cases, suicide. These serious symptoms are caused by huge fluctuations in neurotransmitters and hormones (Brewerton, 1995). Clinical tests have shown that people who settle into a night shift for an extended period and are regularly exposed to bright light at night and darkness during the day can somewhat lessen the damaging effects of this upheaval of the circadian rhythm. (Roberts 2001, 7).

Although scientists continue to study the positive effects of sunlight on the human body, it is clear that the cure for a host of physical and emotional ailments is the biggest, shiniest shiny object of them all—the sun.

Instinctual Attraction

As I mentioned previously, there is very little clinical research available on the reasons why people and other creatures are so drawn to shiny objects. In fact, only in recent years has there been some exploration dedicated to understanding our instinctual attraction to shiny objects.

One of the studies that examined the effects of shiny objects most directly was a two-part study by Richard G. Coss, Department of Psychology, University of California, Davis and Michael Moore, Department of Education in Science and Technology, Technion-Israel Institute of Technology. The basic premise that Coss and

Moore (1990) tested was the notion that over the last 5 million years, the natural selection process has selected only those humans who have the ability to identify sources of drinking water. If this is the case, then humans would exhibit some sort of affinity to water.

In the first part of his study, "All that Glistens: Water Connotations in Surface Finishes," Coss and Moore (1990) tested adults' attraction to glossy and sparkling surfaces. He chose these surfaces because they emulated wet surfaces, such as smooth ponds or shimmering water. Four surfaces were tested: matte, glossy, sandy, and sparkling. Subjects were asked to complete a questionnaire that assessed positive and negative affects connoted by the surface finishes.

Overall, Coss and Moore's results indicated that the adults equated glossy and sparkling surfaces with wetness (with the glossy surface rating the highest). When measured in terms of overall favorable attitudes, the sparkling surface ranked highest, with the glossy surface coming in second. In most cases, women were attracted to the shiny surfaces slightly more than men were. Coss and Moore concluded from these results that "glossy surfaces convey strong optical information about moisture, possibly the result of consistent natural selection over evolutionary time operating on failure to correctly identify mirrored surfaces as water. Preliminary observations of infants selectively mouthing and licking mirrored surfaces support this view" (Coss and Moore 1990, 378). In other words, this part of his experiment supported his initial idea.

In the second part of his study—"All that Glistens: The Effects of Reflective Finishes on the Mouthing Activity of Infants and Toddlers," Coss and colleagues (Coss, Ruff, and Simms 2003) attempted to dig deeper into the apparent natural attraction that infants have for shiny objects. They tested this attraction by observing 46 infants and toddlers between the ages of 7 and 24 months in three age groups. The infants and toddlers were put into a room with two plates: one was white plastic and the other was stainless steel.

The results of the second part of this study showed that approximately 50 percent of the infants mouthed some part of the metal plate, compared to about 25 percent who opted for the plastic plate. In addition, 25 percent of the infants between 6 and 12 months mouthed the center of the metal plate, while none mouthed the center of the plastic plate. Even more curious, about 15 percent of that same group got on their hands and knees to lick the metal plate on the floor (as a person might lap water from a pool), while only about 1 percent of the same group reacted the same way to the plastic plate.

Coss et al. surmise that the results of these experiments seem to indicate that "mouthing activity is indeed influenced early in development by the clarity of reflections and intensity of gleaming highlights on surface finishes that arguably characterize the optical cues for water and wet surfaces" (Coss et al. 2003, 210). In other words, babies demonstrate an attraction to shiny objects because the objects instinctually remind them of water.

In my opinion, these two studies by Coss and colleagues constitute landmark research. They suggest that over the eons of time, only the people who had a natural affinity for water survived. This affinity is present today in our attraction to shiny objects. It is something that all humans have in common and cuts across all races and cultures.

Psychological Attraction

Shiny objects attract us because they relate to the ways in which we meet our very our basic needs. As our needs change, so do our shiny objects. Sometimes our needs are very primitive, like those for food and shelter. At other times, we crave a higher order of needs that include social acceptance and love.

In 1943, Abraham Maslow published his famous "Hierarchy of Needs" in which he attempted to rank order people's needs.

According to Maslow, we have to fulfill our basic needs before we can move up the hierarchy to satisfy higher needs. In other words, if a person is starving or freezing to death, he or she is not going to be terribly concerned about self-esteem. In fact, otherwise civilized people have turned to *very* uncivilized means to survive. One of the most widely publicized cases occurred in Chile in 1972, when 16 members of a Uruguayan soccer team survived for 70 days by consuming their dead teammates after their airliner crashed in the Andes Mountains.

Very few of us will ever have to experience such extreme circumstances. But what about a job layoff or the death of a spouse? In these crisis situations, we typically have to take a step downward and take care of our lower-level needs before we can get back on top. Figure 3.1 is Maslow's depiction of these needs as a pyramid, with the more basic, survival needs creating the foundation and the developmental needs on top.

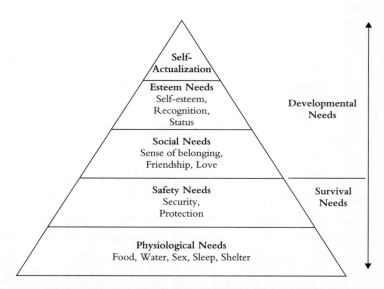

Figure 3.1   Maslow's Hierarchy of Needs

Physiological Needs

Breathing, food, water, sex, sleep, shelter, warmth, homeostasis, and excretion are the needs that all animals have in common and will resort to drastic measures to fulfill. Unfortunately, there are many places in the world where people spend most of their days trying to fill these needs, and they rarely reach a higher level. However, even a person living in the most posh apartment in Manhattan must meet these needs regularly, or they will find themselves in a crisis. We frequently become highly susceptible to these needs as our day-to-day, hour-to-hour circumstances change. For example, early in my career, I produced large-scale meeting presentations using multiple projectors, pyrotechnics, and elaborate stage props. Typically, all hell would break loose three days before a presentation was scheduled. Props were not delivered on time, video editing was not finished, electronics were malfunctioning, and so on. One show in Las Vegas went particularly awry. I had been working for three days straight, without any sleep, trying to pull things together. Once the opening extravaganza was over, I dragged myself up to my room to rest. The last thing I remember was walking into my room. I woke up 24 hours later on the floor. Although I was a strapping young man of 29, my body and mind had finally had enough. My primal need for sleep overrode all else.

Safety Needs

Security and protection of body, employment, resources, morality, the family, health, and property are the needs found on the second level. At this level in the pyramid, we are only slightly divergent from the rest of the animal kingdom. Everyone knows how fiercely a lioness will protect her cubs. People are basically the same; the only difference is in the things we will protect. While a dog will snarl to protect its food bowl, only humans snarl to protect their employment. And only humans will kill other humans to protect yet *other* humans from being killed. Safety needs become extremely strong "shiny objects" when people yearn to fulfill them.

Social Needs

Friendship, sense of belonging, family, and sexual intimacy needs make up the third pyramid level. At this level, we leave most the rest of the animal kingdom behind. While the majority of other animals often congregate in gangs or packs, they do so out of a need for protection or to facilitate hunting. There are a few exceptions, however. Most primates, such as chimpanzees and orangutans, often form social units simply to be with others of their own kind. The "sense of belonging" or "being part of the group" is a very strong shiny object that masters of persuasion have exploited for thousands of years. Consider the term "the chosen people" used throughout the Old Testament. By definition, if there is a group of chosen people, then there must be a group of nonchosen people. If you believe it is God who is doing the choosing, which group would you want to join? And once you are part of the chosen people, the ultimate punishment would be banishment or to be labeled an unbeliever. Modern advertising uses friendship and being part of the group as a mainstay. In fact, the majority of TV commercials utilize this shiny object to some degree to create a feeling of product acceptance or peer pressure. Advertisers want to convince you to become one of the chosen people who own a certain television, wear specific clothes, or drive a particular car.

Esteem Needs

Self-esteem, confidence, achievement, respect of others, and respect by others fall near the top of the pyramid. This is where we completely separate ourselves from the other creatures on earth.

Only humans will expend tremendous resources to achieve some sort of notoriety. While other animals simply don't care, humans certainly do. People have created entire industries around the notion of building self-esteem and confidence. To many, the greatest sense of accomplishment possible is to be held up as an example of success by their peers. To see how prevalent our burning need to be recognized is, do a Google search on the word "respect." At the time of writing this, I got over 342 million hits on "respect." Compare that to 150 million for "Christ" or 91 million for Allah. It speaks volumes about that particular shiny object, doesn't it?

Self-Actualization

Morality, creativity, spontaneity, problem solving, lack of prejudice, and acceptance of facts constitute the pinnacle of the pyramid. At the apex of the pyramid, we find the needs required to reach our fullest potential. Indeed, these needs account for some of mankind's noblest endeavors. Maslow describes self-actualized people in the following way:

- They embrace the facts and realities of the world (including themselves) rather than denying or avoiding them.
- They are spontaneous in their ideas and actions.
- They are creative.
- They are interested in solving problems; this often includes the problems of others. Solving these problems is often a key focus in their lives.
- They feel a closeness to other people and generally appreciate life.
- They have a system of morality that is fully internalized and independent of external authority.
- They have discernment and are able to view all things in an objective manner.

Developmental Needs versus Survival Needs

To better understand Maslow's needs as they relate to shiny objects, I have broken them into two categories. I call the basic, more physical needs *survival needs*, because they are necessary for our physical survival. We simply cannot live without them. However, we can live without the higher level needs, or *developmental needs,* but we will never progress as human beings without meeting them. We seek to satisfy these needs so that our lives will become more fulfilling.

The rule of thumb for shiny objects is—the lower the need you can stimulate, the more intense the desire will be for the person who needs it. This is not to say that higher-level needs are not highly attractive shiny objects. They certainly can be. But, in the same way that physical needs trump social needs, shiny objects that appeal to someone's basic needs stimulate physical instincts that take over cognitive thinking. This is, of course, assuming the person you're trying to attract is susceptible to that basic need. For example, if you are marketing food to someone who is famished, your product will definitely be a shiny object. Depending on how hungry they are, they might even pull off the road the moment they see your restaurant after hearing your ad on the radio. Hunger, thirst, and shelter are three powerful shiny objects. Try talking philosophy to a person who hasn't eaten for days while you munch away on a double cheeseburger. Chances are, he or she won't hear a word you say.

Higher-level needs require a degree of cognitive thinking; that is, you have to decide that you are going to seek them out. In contrast, the lower-level basic needs are requisite for survival. Whether you join a certain group to gain acceptance is your choice, but when you're hungry you are compelled to eat. Because the higher-level needs are often based on a conscious decision, they are also more compelling for long-term branding. If your shiny object attracts someone because of your product's ability to enhance someone's status—and if that person has an experience that confirms the promise of the shiny object—you will have a long-term customer.

Survival Needs	Developmental Needs
Required to be able to live	Required to make life fulfilling
Based on instinctual response	Require some cognitive decision
Quick to satisfy	Long-term fulfillment
Less discriminating	More discriminating
Take what's available	Loyal to decision
Create strong, immediate response	Creates subtle response over time
Vulnerable to quick changes	Resistant to quick changes

These needs and their associated shiny objects are in a constant tug of war. What is most important to a person throughout an average day might change based on the conditions of the moment. Survival needs can suddenly override the developmental needs, but they never replace them, and vice versa.

Here are a couple of examples. Let's say that it's a hot summer day, and you have developed a driving thirst. Your lips are dry, your throat is burning, and you feel roasted. Your thirst survival need has kicked in and your shiny object is obtaining something wet and refreshing to pour down your throat. You spot a soda-vending machine, drop in your change, and then come to the moment of decision. What soda do you choose? Let's say you're a Dr. Pepper kind of person (in fact, you might even be proud of the fact that you buck the cola trend). In most social gatherings you search for the Dr. Pepper and smugly suck it down while everyone else is drinking their run-of-the-mill Cokes. Your developmental need that drives you to be unique in the crowd might even motivate you to take a pass on soda if your beloved Dr. Pepper isn't available. But today, you feel like you just came out of the Sahara, and there are no Dr. Peppers in the machine, only Cokes. What do you do? Do you take a deep breath and trudge on to find another machine? If your thirst is strong enough, your shiny object to quench your thirst is brighter than your shiny object to stand out in a crowd. You go for the Coke and forsake your love of Dr. Pepper. The point is that, depending on the setting, either your survival or developmental need takes control—and your shiny object in each case may be entirely different.

Let's talk about fulfilling a powerful developmental need and discuss the church of Apple for a moment. At my advertising agency, we have both PCs and Macs. I use whichever one best suits my needs for a particular purpose. Sure, I see some advantages on one side of the fence or the other, but at the end of the day, to me, PCs and Macs are both just computers. However, I wouldn't dare make such a blasphemous comment in the creative department. I would be risking an impassioned rebuke on the almost holy attributes of the Mac. In reality, Apple has done a magnificent job of relating to the developmental need of creating a sense of belonging by creating platform warfare (read: "Crusade"). They have convinced a narrow group of people that it is akin to selling their souls to the devil to cross over to the dark side of the PC. In the end, it isn't so much the specifications or tangible benefits of working with a Mac (and there definitely are some) that is important to Mac loyalists. It is the them-versus-us attitude that is the shiny object. It is the feeling that you belong to a tribe. It is clearly a cognitive decision that has created a deep-seated product loyalty among Mac fans.

And Apple loves to polish their shiny object to an almost blinding light. Their "Get a Mac" ad campaign that began in 2006 uses two people to depict a Mac and a PC, and it is a blatant appeal to Mac users' shiny objects. In the ad, PC, a somewhat dour and pudgy old guy, sort of bumbles through the spot. Mac, on the other hand, is a hip-looking very condescending dude who always ends up making PC look like a chump. Very passive/aggressive kind of stuff. Who in the world thinks these ads are designed to create a shiny object for PC users? Calling someone a bumbling idiot is definitely not a shiny object. Clearly, these ads will not convince PC users to come into the light. They might appeal to a younger group of teens or 20-somethings who have not yet joined a camp and could be attracted to the shiny object of belonging to a hip tribe. But one thing is very clear: they successfully wave that shiny object in front of Mac users and remind them of their moral superiority. In that sense, the ads are excellent at solidifying customer loyalty.

4 | Shiny Objects in Our Lives

Shiny objects are ever present in our lives. They are all around us, every moment of the day. We are surrounded by tens of thousands of them. However, not all of them attract our attention. In fact, most of them go unnoticed. The reason is that they are only shiny to us if they have personal meaning or relate to our own unique physical or developmental needs.

Many of these shiny objects are literally *shiny*, such as diamonds, stars, gold, silver, new cars, glistening water, crystal glasses, or a million other objects that gleam and shimmer. But most of the shiny objects that actually catch our attention do not have a "shiny" facade. They only appear shiny if they appeal to an intrinsic need inside of us. Take the diamond, for example. You might be inclined to say that the diamond would be a shiny object regardless of the situation. However, what if you were stranded in the desert, dying of thirst, and a diamond and a glass of water were placed before you? Which one would be your shiny object? In that situation, the diamond is suddenly worthless. Even though it is physically shiny, it has no attraction. Your mind would be solely focused on the glass of water.

It is true that some shiny objects have an intrinsic meaning and are used to communicate a specific message. It's not a coincidence that police cars, fire trucks, and ambulances use shiny objects in the form of flashing lights to communicate danger. Even from a distance, these shiny objects attract our attention and create an immediate reaction. Lighthouses use their shiny object to warn ships of treacherous rocks. Wedding rings are shiny objects that communicate a wide array of thoughts that range from "I've found my soul mate," to "He's taken, leave him alone." However, these types of shiny objects are relatively few.

Not All Shiny Objects Glitter

Most shiny objects are not shiny in appearance; rather, they attract our attention and motivate us to grab them because they connect to

35

our innermost personal desires. A good example of a nonshiny shiny object is food. There is nothing *physically* shiny about a freshly baked load of bread. Yet, because of the way it activates the senses and our recollection of how it tastes, it catches our attention when we walk into a room where it's displayed.

When I was about 10 years old, there was a bakery in my town called Helm's Bakery that would deliver freshly baked bread right to my home. The moment that pastel yellow truck pulled up to the curb, every kid in the neighborhood would swarm around it, just waiting for the driver to open the back doors. The scents that would drift out of that truck were heavenly. To this day, that brand has made a significant, lasting impression on me. I can recall with precise detail how the loaves, donuts, and assorted pastries were meticulously lined up on neat, wooden shelves. There was nothing physically shiny about any of this; but when that truck drove up, I could not help but be attracted to it. Other examples of nonshiny shiny objects are nice clothes, a new home, the hottest video game, a new pair of sneakers, a rare book, a beautiful painting, expensive perfume (although these are usually packaged in shiny bottles), the latest power tool—virtually any object that reaches deep into our primal needs and creates a psychological attraction.

Living, Breathing Shiny Objects

Often, the shiniest objects in our lives are people. We experience tremendous attraction to other people and will often go to extraordinary lengths and sacrifice to obtain and keep a connection with them. While it is true that a few people have sacrificed their lives in pursuit of gold, diamonds, and other worldly possessions, thousands have died for other people. Sometimes the pursuit of this shiny object comes in the form of trying to help other people. Other times, it comes from following people who we believe will guide us down the "yellow brick road." People can be so strongly attracted to other people that they attempt to emulate them, right down to their hair, clothes, and speaking style. We even call people that shine above the rest "stars." The really great ones are "superstars."

Children are usually the shiniest objects in the lives of their parents. Everything that children do attracts their mother and father's attention. Many parents would sacrifice their own lives to protect these shiny objects. History is replete with accounts of parents who gave up everything so their children might have better lives. The more these shiny objects shine, the more the parents shine. Parents pay millions of dollars every year to polish these shiny objects: dance lessons, sports, tutors, clothes, music lessons, and college. To a parent bent on making sure their child reaches his or her fullest, shiniest potential, there is no price that is too high to pay. And when parents don't have the money to pay that price, they borrow it. Parents routinely go into heavy debt to provide their children with higher education and other developmental-need fulfillment.

Never underestimate the power of the human shiny object. Men have fought other men for the affection of women. Tall, handsome men typically get higher paying jobs than short ugly ones. The same is true with attractive women. In civil trials, the most attractive party is more likely to win. Celebrities routinely get off the hook in trials, not only because they can afford to hire the best lawyers, but also because the juries can't resist the shiny object. Teachers rate nice-looking children as smarter than their less attractive classmates. Students rate lectures better when the teacher is more attractive. A study conducted in 1998 by Mulford, Orbell, Shatto, and Stockard found that socially desirable characteristics were more often connected with attractive persons than with unattractive persons. This same study found that "because people are more willing to cooperate with others whom they find attractive, initiating a business deal is easier for an attractive person." Additionally, "an attractive person is more likely to make a greater financial gain through any deal he or she might make, because attractive businesspeople can influence potential customers more efficiently than can less attractive businesspeople" (Blount-Nuss, Cate, and Lattimer 2006, 10).

This attraction to the human shiny object can be significantly manipulated. Like putting a coat of wax on a car, otherwise lackluster people can polish themselves to turn themselves into a shiny object. Although we all hate to confess that we can be manipulated by such superficial trappings, it is nonetheless true. Men are, as a whole, attracted to women who wear makeup and dress nicely. "Those who do dress more fashionably tend to more easily attain jobs, and those jobs generally pay more and are more appealing to workers than are jobs more frequently attained by less fashionable dressers" (Blount-Nuss et al. 2006, 10). Evidently, it is true that clothes do make the man (or woman). Social graces also significantly affect our shiny object. Those who speak well and perform well in public situations rate much higher on the attractiveness scale, especially in politics. People generally shy away from a candidate that has a difficult time speaking. We can also make ourselves more attractive by praising others because people love to hear nice things about themselves.

So apparently, the old adage "If you put lipstick on a pig, it is still a pig," is not exactly borne out by research. To the contrary, all research on the effects of attractiveness shows that the average person can significantly increase his or her ability to be a shiny object by applying relatively simple techniques, such as changing dress or speaking styles. It is good to know there is hope for all of us.

Concepts Can Be Shiny Objects

Some of the most motivating shiny objects aren't objects (or even people) at all. They are concepts: ideas that motivate us to take action. Some of these ideas are positive—freedom, family unity, morality, charity, physical achievement, and pursuit of knowledge.

Others can be negative, such as greed, power over other people, and revenge. Depending on our needs and personal orientations, we choose to follow these positive or negative shiny objects. In most cases—because we are human and therefore, fraught with human weaknesses—we usually seek some of both. Whatever the case, ideas and concepts can become all-consuming, highly motivating, and often taken to the extreme.

One of my favorite examples of taking a shiny object to the extreme is embodied in the character Clark Griswold, played by Chevy Chase in the movie *Christmas Vacation* (Checkik and Hughes, 1989). Although this movie is a total work of fiction, the story it tells bears a strong resemblance to my own holiday family gatherings when I was a young boy. In the movie, Clark's shiny object insists on having a "fun, old-fashioned family Christmas." Clark was so focused on this shiny object that no disaster would deter him from reaching it. Despite his best intentions, the Christmas tree burns up, the cat is electrocuted, dinner is ruined, and the house is destroyed by a dog. The coup de grace comes when Clark receives the company bonus that he was planning on spending on a new swimming pool; and it turns out to be a year's enrollment in the Jam-of-the-Month Club. After he explodes and tries to quell his frustrations with several cups of eggnog, the in-laws appear in the foyer with their bags packed, ready to leave. Clark's response is classic:

> Where do you think you're going? Nobody's leaving. Nobody's walking out on this fun, old-fashioned family Christmas. No, no. We're all in this together. This is a full-blown, four-alarm holiday emergency here. We're gonna press on, and we're gonna have the hap, hap, happiest Christmas since Bing Crosby tap-danced with Danny f***ing Kaye. And when Santa squeezes his fat white *** down that chimney tonight, he's gonna find the jolliest bunch of ******** this side of the nuthouse.

Clark ends up letting his obsession about obtaining his shiny object of the perfect Christmas blind him to everything else, which ironically, ends up pushing that shiny object farther away. By the end of the movie, he realizes that shiny object wasn't as shiny as he thought and his true shiny objects are his family.

A more real-life example of an ideal as a shiny object was Abraham Lincoln's (1863) goal of freedom for all men, especially those in slavery. This shiny object ultimately led to the desire for his second shiny object: holding the Union together at all costs. Both shiny objects are intimately woven together in the speech he delivered at the dedication of the Gettysburg cemetery:

> Four score and seven years ago our fathers brought forth on this continent a new nation, conceived in Liberty, and dedicated to the proposition that all men are created equal.
>
> Now we are engaged in a great civil war, testing whether that nation, or any nation, so conceived and so dedicated, can long endure. We are met on a great battle-field of that war. We have come to dedicate a portion of that field, as a final resting place for those who here gave their lives that that nation might live. It is altogether fitting and proper that we should do this. But, in a larger sense, we can not dedicate— we can not consecrate—we can not hallow—this ground. The brave men, living and dead, who struggled here, have consecrated it, far above our poor power to add or detract. The world will little note, nor long remember what we say here, but it can never forget what they did here. It is for us the living, rather, to be dedicated here to the unfinished work, which they who fought here have thus far so nobly advanced. It is rather for us to be here dedicated to the great task remaining before us—that from these honored dead we take increased devotion to that cause for which they gave the last full measure of devotion—that we here highly resolve that these dead shall not have died in vain—that this nation, under God, shall have a new birth of freedom—and that government of the people, by the people, for the people, shall not perish from the earth.

Delivered in less than three minutes, these few lines have become one of the most famous speeches in American history. Despite a divided congress, severe casualties, a highly critical press, and significant personal health problems, Lincoln refused to take his eye off the shiny object. Ultimately, he possessed that shiny object and held the union together in one of the darkest periods of America's democracy.

To Each His Own Shiny Object

One of the important principles of shiny objects is that my shiny object may not be your shiny object. The best example of this principle is found among collectors of *collectables* and in the phrase, "One man's trash is another man's treasure." These shiny objects usually have little to no intrinsic value. The only value these items have is the value people place on them because they want them. Sometimes so badly, they'll pay a fortune to get them.

Take the Honus Wagner baseball card, for example. It's often referred to as the "Holy Grail of baseball cards." Honus Wagner played baseball way back in 1897, so the card is scarce to begin with. Additionally, at the time that he played, baseball cards were made by tobacco companies. Honus didn't want to encourage kids to smoke, so, he insisted that the tobacco company stop making his card. Today, only about 60 Honus Wagner cards exist and only a handful in mint condition. In September 2007, a Honus Wagner card sold for $2.8 million at auction. Here you have a piece of cardboard that has absolutely no real value; yet someone was willing to part with $2,800,000 dollars to get their hands on it. Think about it. If you had no idea what a Honus Wagner baseball card was worth, and you came across one while cleaning out your grandpa's garage, you might just throw it away. $2.8 million dollars right into the trash can! Proof positive that a shiny object's value is usually in the eye of the beholder.

Another great example of an intrinsically worthless object that's a shiny object is the "Tre Skilling Banco yellow" stamp. A postage stamp worth $2.3 million! Coincidentally, the same amount paid for the Honus Wagner card. For its weight and size, it the most valuable object in the entire world. All because somebody working the printing machine back in 1855 in Sweden made a mistake and printed it on yellow stock instead of green. Sure, there's only one copy in existence; but *it's a postage stamp.* $2.3 million! According to the World Bank's (2005, 1) United Nations Development Program Report, that's over 290 times the worldwide average annual income. For a postage stamp! Never underestimate the power of a shiny object.

One of the most unique and dramatic examples of the power of a shiny object and its ability to occasionally defy logic lies with the lowly tulip. This meek and unassuming bulb was the basis of the cultural frenzy and subsequent collapse of a nation's economy. The time was the early 1630s, and the place was Holland. Tulips had been imported to from Turkey as far back as the late 1500s. In 1593, Charles de L'Ecluse created a variety of tulip that was able to tolerate the harsher conditions of Holland and England, and the flower quickly became a coveted status symbol and luxury item. Almost overnight, these seemingly simple plants began to fetch ridiculously high prices. People began to buy and sell them like one might trade high-priced stocks in the NYSE. Almost daily, the prices would rise dramatically. People even started to sell their farms and homes to cash in on the rush. In 1623, a single bulb of a famous tulip variety could cost as much as a thousand Dutch florins, which was almost ten times the average yearly income. By 1634, the country was literally caught in a flower frenzy. People were leaving their jobs and family in search of tulip fortune. Despite warnings from the government that the bubble would eventually burst, people were sacrificing everything they had to buy these shiny objects ("The Tulip Mania" n.d.).

It is interesting to note that these tulips were not really shiny objects to the people trading in them. They were simply relying on the fact that the flowers were shiny objects to other people. They were so sure that the rich and famous would buy these bulbs that they paid staggering prices for them. In 1635, in exchange for the most famous bulb—known as the Semper Augustus—one tulip trader paid 100,000 florins in the form of two wagon loads of wheat, four loads of rye, four fat oxen, eight fat swine, twelve fat sheep, two hogsheads of wine, four barrels of beer, two barrels of butter, 1,000 pounds of cheese, a marriage bed with linens, and a sizable wagon. All for just one tulip ("The Tulip Mania" n.d.).

However, it takes a lot of people craving a shiny object to keep the supply profitable. In the case of the Tulip Frenzy, the crash came swiftly and hit hard. It wasn't that the aristocracy stopped wanting tulips; it was just that the market could no longer bear the price. And just when speculators were starting to feel the pinch on April 27, 1637, the Dutch government issued a decree that tulips and tulip bulbs were products, not investments, and that they had to be bought and sold on that basis. That meant that tulips had to be paid for in cash. The bubble burst (Tarses 1999)!

Overnight, thousands of Dutch—including businessmen, banks, and government leaders—were financially ruined. People were left holding worthless contracts and huge inventories of tulips. Scores of businesses and financial institutions closed their doors, never to reopen. The entire country became instantly impoverished. There were so many bankruptcies that the national treasury was depleted and Holland had to radically reduce its army and navy, as there was no money to pay for them. As a result, it lost many of its colonies such as New Amsterdam, which was taken over by the British and renamed New York. All because an entire nation got caught up in a shiny object frenzy (Tarses 1999).

Shiny Objects Are Always Changing

People's needs—physical, emotional, and otherwise—are constantly changing. As a result, many of their shiny objects are in a constant state of flux. As we move from one chapter of our lives to another, our priorities change and we value things, people, and situations differently.

Even while in the same chapter, events—even small ones—occur that cause us to shift our attention to different shiny objects:

- *Couple has their first child:* There's nothing like a newborn baby to change your perspective on the world. Suddenly, a host of shiny objects appear that you never noticed: car seats, baby swings, baby food, pediatricians, diapers, a good night's sleep, an evening alone with your spouse, and college tuition funds.
- *Death of a spouse:* Suddenly, your entire world changes. Things that you were focused on might now seem inconsequential. Other issues, such as mortality, family, and simple conversations take on a new significance. If you relied on your spouse for a living, another shiny object for you is suddenly finding employment.
- *Elderly parents suddenly need care:* Many baby boomers are finding themselves in the position of being caregivers for their parents. Issues and problems with which they have never dealt in their lives become part of a daily routine. They find themselves much more interested in assisted living facilities, dementia, and the simple act of getting their parents around.
- *A three-month project at work, compressed into one month:* You might have been focused on that ball game next week or that really great restaurant you made reservations for three months in advance. All that goes out the window; and your shiny object now is figuring out how to compact three months into one— and how to have time for eating and sleeping while you're at it.
- *Change of career:* You realize that you are in a dead-end job because you made some bad choices earlier in your career. Your shiny object now becomes your personal job satisfaction and how to change directions in the least amount of time possible.
- *Low fuel warning:* When your gas tank is full, you pass by hundreds of gas stations without paying any attention to them. However, when that low-fuel warning light comes on, you

start noticing gas stations where you never saw them before (or wishing they were where they are *not*). Although they are short term, they become *extremely* shiny objects.

- *Looking for a new car:* On a normal day, one or two cars might catch your eye while you're driving on the freeway; you probably pass thousands of them without a second thought. However, once you've made the decision to buy a new car, suddenly your shiny object shifts, and you start noticing the slightest nuances of all the models that whiz by.

- *Starting a new relationship:* Couples are usually on their best behavior when they first start dating. They dress nicely; they're careful about what they say; they use their best manners; and they try to be as shiny of an object they can be to the other person.

- *Illness:* Typically, we pay absolutely no attention to cold remedies and other health aids when we're in tip-top health. Almost no one goes to the drugstore and loads up on cough syrup and antihistamines just to be prepared. However, once that cold hits, our shiny object becomes crystal clear, and we will go to any length to find a store that's open at 1:00 AM just to get some relief.

- *Your doctor tells you to lose 50 pounds:* You're going along fat, dumb, and happy, until the threat of heart troubles refocuses your shiny object to be just dumb and happy.

- *You just decided to go on a vacation:* You rarely pay any attention to the travel section in the newspaper and would never be caught dead watching the travel channel. However, once you've decided to go on a vacation, these otherwise ignored sources of information become shiny objects. You begin to notice articles about hot travel spots that you would have disregarded before.

- *You need to move:* This is one of the most disruptive chapters in a person's life. You never realize how much of your life is tied to your address until it comes time to change it. Your life is suddenly full of new shiny objects. Picking a mover. Changing the utilities. Transferring the kids to a new school. Finding a new place to get your hair cut. Finding boxes. Preparing the new house. Finding a new doctor for yourself. Finding a new vet for Fifi. Forwarding mail. There are so many issues to deal with—so many shiny objects—that it can be overwhelming.

- *At work, you've been put in charge of finding a new phone system:* The phone system has always been something that's just there. You have never really paid much attention to it except to use it when you need it, or occasionally, to change your outgoing voice message. However, once the boss has given you the task to replace it, your world becomes full of hundreds of phone system options, price lists, and user interfaces. Everyone in the office suddenly has opinions on the subject and it seems that no matter what you choose, you are doomed to fail. Your shiny object becomes anyone or anything that will simplify this task.

- *You just started playing golf and discovered you really like it:* Instantly the most boring channel on cable (the golf channel) becomes a beacon of interest, your travel destinations start to become centered around golf courses, and you become aware of the hundreds of fascinating golf accoutrements that are available at the pro shop.

- *You just broke up with someone:* Depending on whether you are the breaker or the breakee, your shiny objects will be entirely different. Either way, there will be a dramatic shift from where you were before.

- *A presidential election:* You might suddenly become aware of political issues you have not considered. In many cases, these issues might change the way you view your town, your neighbors, the economy, and the world at large. Some people become so attracted to these shiny objects that they volunteer their spare time to help convince others.

Four Shiny Object Principles

The fact that shiny objects are constantly changing does not mean that marketers should throw up their hands in frustration. Despite the fluctuations, successful marketers can depend on four fundamental and consistent principles of shiny objects.

1. Many Shiny Objects Are Deeply Rooted and Resistant to Change

While it is true that thousands of shiny objects are always in a state of flux, there are just as many that do not change very often. For example, providing good health for their children is a shiny object that remains fixed for most parents. In fact, even after children become adults, their parents are still attracted to this shiny object. The need for companionship is another example of a continuous shiny object for most people; whether you are looking for a serious relationship, a friend to spend time with, or even a pet—the need to have some sort of creature by one's side is a strong and fairly constant need. Other examples of fixed shiny objects are the need to have a job and provide an income for yourself, the need for entertainment (whether watching TV, going to the movies, reading a book, or simply walking through the park), the need for a good night's sleep, the need for good health through proper nutrition and exercise, and the need to be safe and secure.

2. At Any Given Time, Many People Are Attracted to the Same Shiny Object

Though an object may be shiny one day and not shiny the next for specific individuals, the law of the masses says that there will always be a certain group of people attracted to the same shiny object at the same time. In fact, if this principle were not true, there would be chaos in the marketplace. If everyone wanted a MacDonald's hamburger at the same time, the restaurant's entire system would break down. If everyone decided to tighten his or her spending belt at the same time, it would destroy the economy. Fortunately, shiny objects have a way of evening themselves out. Many sources of these products, such as fast food restaurants, have discovered that it is necessary to advertise constantly to keep their shiny object out in the marketplace at all times. They never know when their potential customers du jour might see it. Several years ago, as marketing director for a major restaurant chain in Southern California, I was acutely aware that our primary market was made up of people who came to our restaurant no more than once a month. Sure, there was a small group of avid fans that ate there almost daily, but the major portion of our customers was a moving target. There were simply too many choices of possible places to have lunch or dinner. As a result, we had to keep up a fairly heavy promotion schedule. The moment we cut back, we would see a drop in sales.

3. Short-Term Shiny Objects Can Be Extremely Motivating

Desire for short-term shiny objects is usually driven by either some sort of survival need or a fad. In either case, many companies have been very successful at capitalizing on short-term shiny objects that are very fleeting.

There are two successful approaches to these short-term shiny objects:

1. If dealing with a fad, you need to be prepared to get in and get out quickly.
2. If you are going to base your brand on a short-term shiny object, it is be wise to choose one that is cyclical or reoccurs frequently.

Fads In 1993, my advertising agency—along with many other marketing companies—was involved with a fad that became a global phenomenon. It centered on a game called POG, where players collected milk bottle caps and then challenged others to see if they could win their POGs in a fashion similar to playing marbles. POG—which stood for Passion fruit Orange Guava—was a brand of bottled fruit drink manufactured and sold by Haleakala Dairy in Maui. The game used the milk bottle caps of this drink, but it had actually started in 1920 when dairy workers used milk bottle caps in a similar game. Blossom Galbiso, a teacher at Waialua Elementary School on the north shore of Oahu, is credited with reviving the game in 1991. She began using the milk caps in her classroom and used the game of POG to help her teach mathematics to her students. The game begins by stacking the milk caps facedown. The players take turns throwing their *slammer* (a thicker, heavier POG also called a "kini") down onto the top of the stack, causing it to spring up and the POGs to scatter. Each player keeps any POGs that land faceup after his or her throw. After each throw, the POGs that have landed facedown are then restacked for the next player. When no POGs remain in the stack, the player with the most POGs is the winner. All players keep any POGs that they have collected (if playing for keeps) or redistribute them to their original owners.

The game quickly became popular in elementary and junior high schools throughout Hawaii and made its way to the continental United States. From there, the game spread throughout the world like wildfire. At one point, there was actually a World POG Federation that licensed the name from the Haleakala Dairy and had three international branches: The United Kingdom (the original World POG Federation), United States, and Australia.

Recognizing the huge demand, hundreds of companies jumped into the market and started producing and selling POGs to capitalize on their popularity. McDonald's, Burger King, Carl's Jr., and other fast food restaurant chains gave away free POGs with the purchase of a menu item. Fox television reportedly released a line of POGs with the debut of the animated TV series *The Tick*. Disneyland produced limited edition milk caps for its "Go POG Wild and Rollerblade Crazy" event in the spring of 1994. Other companies that jumped onto the bandwagon included Coca Cola, Mattel, the NFL, Upper Deck, Twentieth Century Fox, Universal Studios, Campbell Soup, Warner Brothers, DC Comics, GE/Sanyo, and even The Tournament of Roses. Knott's Berry Farm produced a limited edition set for the 1994 Southern California POG Championship. POG play became so popular that there was a U.S. National POG Tournament held every February 7th from 1993–1997, in honor of the game's inventor's birthday.

At the early stage of this fad, our advertising agency recognized the potential for using it in sales promotions and encouraged our clients to capitalize it. Those who did so had significant success. However, at the same time, we could see that this type of explosive popularity could not sustain itself very long, and so we constructed very short-term promotions. We knew that we had to get in fast and get out fast.

Sure enough, the POG bubble burst. A very enterprising young man—Marcus Riddington of Murphreesburg, Pennsylvania—accompanied his family on a trip to Las Vegas, Nevada in November of 1995 for a Thanksgiving holiday. This was back in the days when Las Vegas was attempting to promote itself as a family destination. While there, he observed his parents and other adults having a lot of fun playing games and winning money at the same time. He figured, "Why not find a way to gamble with POGs?" It wasn't long after he returned home that the students of Murphreesburg Middle School were wagering not only inventory from their own POG collections, but actual money as well. Despite the negative reaction by the school—the decision to ban POG playing on the school grounds—the gambling trend spread across the nation as quickly as the original game. That was its death knell.

Almost overnight, Haleakala Dairy, concerned about negative connotations associated with the gambling wave, sued to prevent manufacturers from using the name POG in any packaging or marketing materials. The company even switched from bottles to cartons to further distance themselves from the game. Parents began to confiscate POGs from their kids, and almost every school district across the country banned the game. Several companies tried to keep the craze going by offering similar products under the names of Tazos and Slammer Whammers, but by 1998, the game's popularity was dead.

While they lasted, POGs were terrific shiny objects.

The list of shiny object fads is almost endless. To name a few: Atkins diet, Beanie Babies, Pet Rocks, tie-dye, Furbys, Digital Pets, mood rings, Cabbage Patch Kids, lava lamps, Droodles, Pokemon, Troll dolls, and the Hula Hoop. Oh by the way—toy manufacturers made over $45 million in less than 12 months on the hula hoop. There is certainly nothing wrong with latching onto a short-term shiny object; but you need to recognize it won't last forever and be prepared to drop it fast.

Recurring Short-Term Shiny Objects Many shiny objects have a short shelf life, but they return again and again. Some are extremely cyclical and predictable. Even though they are short-term, these types of shiny objects make excellent foundations for branding because of their predictability. Many of these temporary shiny objects are aligned with survival needs. They can have a strong, primal attraction. But once fulfilled, they almost instantly fade away. Successful brands that rely on these types of shiny objects find ways to either shorten the cycle or align their marketing timing with it.

As evidence of the enduring nature of survival needs as a shiny object, of the 100 oldest companies in the world—dating all the way back to AD 578—36 are food related (restaurants, bakeries, confectionaries), 10 are clothing related (shoes, fabrics, tailors), and

7 are shelter related (hotels, inns, and taverns) ("The 100 Oldest Companies in the World" 2008).

Food For the most part, food is not a shiny object in the course of our daily lives. It is not at the forefront of our mind as we partake in day-to-day activities. In fact, many people don't think about it much at all. They eat when they have to, and meals get in the way of the rest of their activities. There are times in fact, after we've eaten a big meal, that food can actually be repulsive—the very antithesis of a shiny object. However, the majority of people get hungry at some point in the day and when they do, food becomes a shiny object. For those who have a craving or have gone without food for a period of time, a meal can be an almost blinding shiny object. People in this state can often think of nothing else until they satiate this survival need. The odd thing is that once attained, this shiny object immediately diminishes and is almost extinguished until the next time we get hungry.

However, restaurants, markets, and other food vendors can rely on the fact that our bodies continue to need food. No matter how much we mean it when we say after gorging ourselves on Thanksgiving Day, "I'll never eat again as long as I live," that shiny object comes back the very next day.

Cold Remedies Companies that manufacture cold remedies fully understand that their product is seasonal. Sure, people experience the occasional summer cold, but the really bad stuff gets revved up every winter. These companies make a very tidy profit (approximately $4 billion a year) hanging out this shiny object during "the cold and flu season." While they continue to run a meager maintenance advertising program throughout the rest of year, the bulk of their campaigns occur during the winter.

Coincidentally, while writing this book, I caught a terrible cold. I don't get sick very often, but when I do, I feel miserable. I have to have my DayQuil and NyQuil right now! The rest of the time I could care less. But when I'm sick, I grab the coupon pages out of the newspaper and clip out some miracle cure that will make me feel better. Basically, I'm a wimp; and when I'm sick, there is no object shinier than a cold remedy.

Although it is a few years old, "a week-by-week comparison of ACNielsen sales data with flu statistics from the Centers for Disease Control (CDC)" compiled in 2004 "shows that sales of OTC cough and cold remedies rise and fall roughly in synch with the onset and decline of the flu season." In each of the three years studied (2001, 2002, and 2003), "weekly sales of cough and cold remedies peaked at levels between $120 and $170 million from December to March, declined gradually in the spring, and bottomed out at around $60 million between June and August. Early September through late November typically sees a gradual rise to sales of $80 to $120 million per week" (Lempert 2004).

The list of products that do extremely well with seasonal shiny objects is enormous—and it includes such items as suntan lotion, grass seed and fertilizer, back-to-school supplies, seasonal clothing, ski and snowboarding equipment, and holiday items. The primary issue with these types of seasonal items is not so much the duration of the season, but how well prepared the company is to get the shiny object out in plain view in time to capitalize on the brevity of interest.

Fashion   Whereas cold remedies and suntan lotions are based on naturally occurring cycles, other shiny objects are created around artificial cycles; but very definite ones, nonetheless. At the top of the list in this category is fashion. Apparel wears out every year, whether you physically wear it out or not. It simply becomes obsolete because something new comes out. And it is expected that something new will always come out.

The idea that fashion follows a man-made cycle is nothing new. Over 50 years ago, Quentin Bell, a sociologist and professor of fine art at Oxford University, Hull University, and University of Sussex wrote a book entitled *On Human Finery*. In this book, he theorized that fashion follows a cyclical phase based on studying dress patterns in Western society for over 600 years.

It seems that fashion designers are part magicians who create a mass hypnosis among millions of people, convincing them that they need to give up their perfectly good clothing because a brand new shiny object has appeared on the stage. Every season, they try to convince us that their awe-inspiring fashions from last year are somehow outdated, boring, and simply dreary. To enjoy the best life has to offer, you must abandon the obsolete and embrace the fresh. How can a fashion that is described as "pushing the limits" or even "going beyond the edge of shocking" be downgraded to "dull and innocuous" in a scant 12 months? Are we really that schizophrenic? Or do we simply join in the cycle of fashion because it promises something brand new every year, and with that, a type of new beginning?

Whatever the reason, an entire industry with sales over $180 billion depends heavily on this annual cycle. The key to success in the fashion industry is to convince your market that your shiny object is vastly shinier than the one last year. In fact, you have to be downright brazen about how shiny the new object is and how the old shiny object no longer shines at all.

4. Most Shiny Objects Evolve Rather than Change Abruptly

The good news for marketers is that most shiny objects don't change overnight. Instead, they slowly evolve from one form to another. This usually gives astute marketers enough time to adapt. The challenge is that they need to recognize changing shiny objects so that they don't get caught talking to themselves in an empty room.

Get Out of the Fast Lane or Get Run Over   An example of an industry that did not adapt to the idea of evolving shiny objects is the U.S. auto industry. It might seem harsh to heap another criticism on the U.S. auto industry, and for that I apologize. But, there is simply no greater example in our country's history than this of how a few people's refusal to follow the evolving shiny object has had such a tremendous and long-term impact on the lives of so many people.

After World War II, the U.S. economy saw unprecedented growth. The boys were home, and everyone wanted to forget the war and get on with life—the bigger, the better. The cars that the U.S. auto industry was making at the time seemed to be the perfect reward for a bounding economy. First of all, the automakers had more than doubled their production capacity during wartime, giving them the ability to pump out a lot of cars. Second, the new interstate highway system was being planned and was just about ready to connect the entire country with a network of crisscrossing thoroughfares. The cars were shiny, huge, powerful, and comfortable. Sure, they drank shiploads full of gas, but who cared? Gas was only 26 cents a gallon, and there was no such thing as OPEC. We not only produced almost every vehicle purchased in the United States, but our cars became the symbol for decadence worldwide. It was a great ride. The engines got bigger and more powerful. By 1955, in just eight years, sales went from 4.8 million units to 7.2 million. And U.S. automakers seemed to act like it would never change (Wright 1996).

Well, unfortunately, some shiny objects do have a habit of changing. The first move was somewhat subtle. Volkswagen introduced its beetle to the United States in the 1950s. Initially, its sales were poor. However, due to persistent, quality advertising, the cars slowly began to gain popularity with the U.S. market.

The next change was not so subtle. The Organization of Petroleum Exporting Countries (OPEC) was formed in 1960 with five founding members: Iran, Iraq, Kuwait, Saudi Arabia, and Venezuela. Their stated objective was to control oil prices. At the time, U.S. automakers obviously paid no heed to their threat.

The next change came right on the heels of OPEC. Japan automakers watched the steady growth of Volkswagen and realized there was a significant market for small cars. The shiny object had changed for millions of people from big to small. Small cars were no longer equated with poor quality. They were viewed as cute and cool. However, U.S. automakers did not consider Japanese car manufacturers to be a threat to them in the small car market.

Imported cars, with lower prices and better fuel efficiency became very popular in the 1970s, due in part to the rising cost of gasoline. Then, a catastrophic change occurred in 1973. In a show of strength, OPEC cut off the supply of oil to the United States. Gas prices skyrocketed almost overnight. Foreign automakers of small import cars, especially the Japanese cars, were in a perfect situation to take advantage of the crisis. They had the advantage of better industry-government collaboration, newer factories, and a comparatively cheaper, more disciplined labor force. Toyota and Nissan eventually passed Volkswagen in sales in the United States in 1975 and 1976. By the end of the 1970s, Japanese automakers were selling 2.5 million cars a year in the United States, which amounted to about one of every four units sold (Wright 1996).

By this time, U.S. automakers were trying to follow the shiny object. The problem was that they were two shiny objects behind. They were just starting to figure out how to make small cars, while the shiny object had now moved to exotic features like moon roofs, remote access trunk lids, and powered radio antennas.

Then the shiny object moved again. People in the United States no longer wanted just small cars. They wanted small cars with quality. At this point, the Japanese built their reputation on cars that seems to last forever. And then another change: the Japanese introduced luxury cars—Acura, Infiniti, and Lexus. While they were breaking all sales records, the U.S. automakers were still several shiny objects behind, just starting to introduce popular features into their cars.

In July 2007, foreign automakers outperformed U.S. companies in the U.S. market for the first time ever. And in the first quarter of 2007, General Motors (GM) lost its dominance in the worldwide market to Toyota. Toyota sold 2.35 million vehicles during that period compared with GM's 2.26 million vehicles. Toyota was expected to overtake GM as the world's largest car and light truck maker by the end of the year. U.S. automakers continued to close plants in the United States and lay off workers, while foreign car companies continued to open plants in the United States (Wright 1996).

It wasn't as though the Japanese auto industry had an inside track on the moving shiny object. U.S. automakers had access to all the same information Japanese automakers had. The difference is that Japanese automakers moved to follow the shiny object while U.S. automakers refused to believe that it even existed.

Shiny Object Ahoy!

Now, for an example of an industry that successfully evolved with the shiny object: the cruise industry.

Ever since they were floated, ships have carried passengers. Even ships that were designed to strictly carry cargo or troops have been conscripted into carrying passengers from time to time. However, the first true passenger ship line that was organized strictly to carry people for prolonged distances was the Peninsula and Oriental Steam Navigation Company in 1844. The line, know as P&O, ran ships from Britain to Spain and Portugal to Malay and China. Later, P&O organized trips to Malta, Turkey, Greece, and Egypt. One of the earliest known American-origin cruises was the 1867 voyage of the paddle wheel steamer, *Quaker City*, from New York to the Holy Land, Egypt, and Greece. Mark Twain (1869, 23) made this voyage famous in his book, *The Innocents Abroad*. In the book, Twain described the six-month journey as "a picnic on a gigantic scale." The idea that one could visit a number of different far away places in comparative ease and safety was relatively new, and quickly became popular (Twain 1869, 19).

Commerce between Europe and North American picked up steam in the early 1900s, and thousands began booking travel across the Atlantic. Most of these passengers did not travel in opulent luxury as some of the ships are pictured. While it is true that the elite traveled in grand style, the primary shiny object of the day was being able to safely and economically travel across the second largest and most dangerous ocean in the world. It was the primary mode of transportation between continents.

The first major shift in the shiny object for travel came in the late 1950s when carriers such as Pan Am and TWA introduced jet passenger planes. For the first time it became practical to travel between continents by air. Suddenly people were attracted by the speed and economy by which they could travel long distances. Why be cooped up on a ship for a week when you could get there in a few hours by air?

Since the airlines now owned the transportation market, the savvy cruise industry changed their shiny object from transportation to leisure travel. In fact, many shipping lines added passenger quarters to their freighters and began offering the public extended trips to exotic locations. This approach was met with tremendous success.

The next shiny object shift came when the cruise line operators realized that there was a larger potential market that might be interested if the trips were shorter. As a result, the 1960s saw shipping lines offering shorter (7 to 10 days) and more moderately priced Caribbean cruises from new homeports in South Florida. The first cruise ships designed specifically to be cruise ships were the invention of Ted Arison, who offered cruises from Miami to Caribbean with two ships, *Sunward* and *Starward*, under the name of Norwegian

Caribbean Lines (NCL). The concept was so successful that the market started to grow and quickly attracted competition. In 1967, a group of Norwegian and American investors started up a new future giant: Royal Caribbean Cruise Lines (RCCL), which soon launched a modern fleet of vessels destined for year-round Caribbean sailings from Miami (Henderson 2005).

By the 1970s, the industry realized that the shiny object had shifted again. It wasn't just the destinations that were the draw, it was the ships themselves. In fact, even though the cruise was designed to stop at several alluring ports along the way, many people never left the comfort of the ship. At that point, the optimum ship was considered to be 20,000 tons with a passenger count of 800. Today, most cruise ships are well over 100,000 tons and carry over 5,000 passengers. At the time of this printing, Royal Caribbean has ordered the largest cruise ship ever. Scheduled to set sail in 2009, the *Genesis* will weigh in at 220,000 tons and carry 5,400 passengers. These new breeds of cruise ships truly are floating cities and offer a complete vacation without ever having to leave the deck ("Genesis Class" n.d.).

With all these moving shiny objects and fluctuating economies, the cruise industry has managed to continually post successful years. The Florida-Caribbean Cruise Association (CLIA) forecasted a record 12.6 million passengers in 2007, representing an increase of 0.5 million guests over 2006, which equals a 4.1 percent yearly growth. As a testament to continued growth, between 2007 and 2010, the CLIA-member cruise lines will invest $15.2 billion in 29 state-of-the-art new ships Florida-Caribbean Cruise Association (n.d.).

Not bad for an industry that was supposed to be dry-docked with the advent of jet travel. The secret of its success has been constantly watching the shiny object, and not being afraid to change its industry as the shiny object changes.

5 | Traditional Persuasion Theory versus Shiny Objects

I'm not going to spend a whole lot of space here discussing traditional persuasion theory. The whole reason I developed Shiny Objects Marketing was to provide a simpler alternative to the traditional approach. However, sometimes ideas are best understood by contrasting them with what they are not.

The purpose of presenting Shiny Objects Marketing is not to suggest that modern persuasion theory doesn't work; it actually works quite well. There have been volumes of research dedicated to proving this point. Shiny Objects Marketing is presented as an alternative and simpler way to look at the challenge of motivating people to action. Humans are highly complex entities, and the decision-making process can be quite complicated and involved. I developed Shiny Objects Marketing as a way to cut through those layers of complexity and appeal directly to a person's instincts.

Most modern advertising is based on traditional persuasion theory. The premise of this approach is that people found their purchasing decisions on their beliefs and values. To convince someone to buy something, you must overcome the attitudes created by those beliefs and values or use them to your advantage.

There are two basic persuasion models. One is internally based and the other external.

Internal Persuasion Model

Values → Beliefs → Thoughts → Actions

This model is based on the premise that ultimately our actions are dictated by what goes on inside our heads—our values. Every person has a deep-seated set of values that develop over many years and are resistant to change. These values determine the belief system that we create internally to support our values. Our beliefs generate and guide our thoughts. At the very least, our beliefs filter the way we see things, and therefore, dictate our thoughts. Ultimately, our thoughts dictate our actions. The old adage "You are what you think" is absolutely true. As James Allen wrote in his timeless classic in 1902, *As a Man Thinketh:*

Mind is the Master power that moulds and makes,
And Man is Mind, and evermore he takes
The tool of Thought, and, shaping what he wills,
Brings forth a thousand joys, a thousand ills:
He thinks in secret, and it comes to pass:
Environment is but his looking-glass. (p. 1)

Here's an example of the internally based model: suppose you have been raised to believe that smoking is morally bad. Based on that value, you are prone to believe any negative information on smoking. You might even believe that secondhand smoke can kill people, without reading a word of research on the subject. This belief causes you to think that people should not be allowed to smoke in public places. Along comes a ballot initiative banning smoking on city streets and you take action by voting for the measure.

External Persuasion Model

Sensory Input → Thoughts → Beliefs → Attitudes → Actions

This model focuses on how external factors can influence our actions. It begins with sensory input, such as images, sounds, words, feelings, tastes, and odors. Our mind grinds all of this up and produces thoughts in reaction to the stimuli. If repeated and channeled into a specific direction, these thoughts—either consciously or subconsciously—create our set of beliefs. Based on these beliefs, we form attitudes about the world around us and whether we accept the sensory input as acceptable or not. These attitudes, in turn, prescribe our actions.

For example, suppose it is an election year, and you take the time to listen to one of the candidate's speeches. His words cause you to consider the issue he is bantering about. Perhaps the first time you heard his slogan, it went right by you, barely noticed. But after hearing it and seeing it several hundred times, you begin to think there might be something to it. All this thinking eventually leads you to the belief that, doggone it, he's absolutely right. This belief grows into a steadfast attitude that filters all the opposing viewpoints, and you begin to see the world in the same way the candidate does. This attitude leads to a host of actions: you engage your brother-in-law in political debate, you forward e-mails that support your candidate's position, and you ultimately vote for him.

Shiny Objects Model

Sensory Input → Reactions → Thoughts → Actions

Shiny objects supersede beliefs and values because they appeal to a deeper set of reflexes and instincts that are encoded into our DNA. Sensory input creates an immediate response, without having to filter anything through beliefs and values. For example, when you tap your knee just right, your leg reflectively kicks up. It doesn't have to evaluate the tap according to how you view the world or what your current attitude is about being tapped on the knee. All your leg knows is that it has to kick. It *has* to kick. It has no alternative. Once the kick has occurred, you will most likely think about it. "Hmmm, that was interesting. I think I'll try it again." So, the immediate reaction stimulates thoughts that lead to further action.

Don't Think about It

The big difference between traditional theory and Shiny Objects Marketing is the notion of cognitive response. Traditional persuasion theory assumes that people think prior to acting. While this is true in many cases, it is certainly not a universal truth. The fact is we make millions of responses each day without a single thought crossing our minds.

According to the cognitive response theorists, a person's mental reactions to a message play a critical role in the persuasion process, typically an even more important role than the message itself. In other words, the baggage we bring with us makes the primary decision of whether we respond to a certain message. This theory is the basis for the Elaboration Likelihood Model (ELM), which focuses on how a person elaborates on the message they are receiving. In this model, there are two levels of how we process messages.

The first process is called the *central process*, which is a procedure that requires considerable cognitive thinking. A typical reaction to a message at this level would be, "Let me think about that for a minute." Then we take the message and process it through our values, beliefs, and attitudes in a very cognitive way. We judge the message based on its merits as we see them. For instance, we might react by saying, "Well, according to what I know, that just won't work." Or we could react favorably by saying something like, "Of course! That makes perfect sense." In both cases, we elaborate on the message at hand by adding our own perception to it.

The second process is called the *peripheral process*. In this process, we elaborate on the message based on peripheral factors that have absolutely nothing to do with the message itself. These peripheral factors include the speaker's appearance, their speaking style, and their expertise or notoriety. They also include factors such as music, colors, and images. This type of process is usually very quick. We make a snap judgment based on these peripheral cues. Modern advertising is replete with persuasion using the peripheral process. Whether it is a football player pitching real estate or the music of a famous rock band used to make a certain car seem more appealing, peripheral cues can be very effective. In fact, many of these cues are used to make a shiny object even shinier, which we'll discuss in Chapter 9.

Shiny Objects Marketing short circuits cognitive response by removing the cognitive processes. Although it is certainly true that the ELM actually works, Shiny Objects Marketing is designed to work on a more instinctual level.

Leave Your Attitude at the Door

Most modern persuasion theory focuses on overcoming or appealing to a person's attitudes. Richard M. Perloff, considered by many to be the foremost authority on persuasion, wrote in his book *The Dynamics of Persuasion:* "If you understand the factors impinging on someone and how he or she thinks about a persuasive message, you have a good chance of devising a message that will target the individual's attitudes" (Perloff 2003, 146). This is clearly the case if you accept the fact that all persuasion must be done on a cognitive level. If you can bypass attitudes—and as a result, bypass most traditional persuasion theory—then you can go right to the instinctive level.

If you accept the premise that you must overcome attitudes before persuading a person to take a specific action, then you also must accept the often-complicated process of developing a message that accomplishes that goal. Alternatively, if you base your message on a shiny object, you need only concern yourself with finding that shiny object—which is usually much simpler.

Most modern psychologists and sociologists, including Darwin and Freud, have delved into the world of attitudes to better understand the human psyche. Darwin felt attitudes were more instinctually based. In his work *Expression of the Emotions in Man and Animals,* Darwin defines attitude as a "biological mobilization to respond." He describes attitude as largely a motor function; for example, a scowling face signifies a hostile attitude. Later psychologists began to believe that attitudes were more cognitive in nature and were a learned behavior. Freud endowed attitudes with personality and aligned them with human emotions such as longing, hatred, love, passion, and prejudice (Allport 1935, 801).

Shiny Objects Marketing is based on instincts rather than on cognitive processes and is more in line with Darwin's thinking than Freud's. However, Shiny Objects Marketing accepts both points of view. While many of our attitudes are the result of learned behavior, there is a layer of instinctual response that we don't even think about. We simply react to stimuli.

Comparison of Attitudes versus Shiny Objects

Attitudes	Shiny Objects
Learned	Instinctual
Regionally based	Universal
Product of environment	Product of DNA
Influence thoughts and actions	Motivate action without thought

Read Me First

Why in the world would I entitle a section in the middle of the book, "Read Me First"? Well, actually, I toyed with the idea of putting this right up front, but I decided it would make more sense after a discussion of traditional persuasion theory. However, this is an extremely critical point I am about to make. If the reader doesn't fully grasp this concept, then the balance of the book will be worthless to them. Once we leave this section, we will move into aligning your brand with the shiny object principles. If you are out of sync with the concept, that alignment won't happen.

Forget, for a moment, everything you've ever learned about selling features and benefits. I promise to let you have back all your traditional theories if you just let go for a moment—even though you may discover that once you let go, you might not want to go back. So, let go of every buzzword, catchphrase, or bullet point you've ever used to convince someone to purchase your product or service. Let it all go. In place of that feature/benefit list, I want you to think in terms of survival and developmental needs. To put it succinctly, everything we buy fulfills a need. Shiny Objects Marketing depends on you being in tune with those needs that drive your sales.

As part of our product offering, my advertising agency, AdMatrix, conducts Shiny Objects Workshops. The objective of the workshop is to take the teachings in this book and help the client put them into day-to-day practice. At one of the first workshops I conducted, I learned a valuable lesson. Somehow, I had not communicated that the whole reason that Shiny Objects Marketing works on an instinctual level is that it taps into primal needs—the survival and developmental type. We spent about three and a half hours going through the philosophy of shiny objects, the psychological and physiological basis for shiny object attraction and how Shiny Objects Marketing compares with traditional persuasion theory. Things were going great! The participants were participating, the presenters were presenting, and everyone seemed to be really getting a lot out of the workshop. Then it came time to start identifying shiny objects that were specific to their company.

I was a little surprised, at first, by their suggestions. Instead of concepts that related to basic needs, they began a litany of standard features and benefits. As we moved along, hoping that they would at some point get the idea, my surprise turned to frustration. Eventually, I tried to get them to reach deeper into their ideas, to look at the basic need behind each benefit, but this only served to frustrate them.

For example, I probed to see if the products the company sold helped people get promotions. One person in the room authoritatively stated, "Promotions? We don't have anything to do with job promotions." When I pressed the subject, the rest of the room agreed and insisted that they had absolutely no impact on promotions. However, by the end of the session, it was very clear that those customers that utilized their products saw significantly positive effects in their own companies. Those positive effects became very visible to top leadership positions and often resulted in a promotion.

The fact is I screwed up. I underestimated the hold that traditional thinking has on people. How hard it is to (dare I say it) think outside the box, especially in a group setting. Some of the people in the room were experts at selling their product, and they were absolutely convinced that it was the product's features and benefits—along with their sales skills—that were selling the product. Ultimately, we were able to peel back the layers of benefitspeak and get to some very exciting shiny objects; but it was an ordeal. The people that had been with the company the longest had the hardest time letting go. Conversely, the person who caught the vision the fastest and started right in with real shiny objects had only been with the company for one day. She knew virtually nothing of the company culture. She only knew that the product appealed to some very intrinsic needs that didn't show up on any feature or benefit list.

A few weeks after that first workshop, I had a follow-up mini-workshop with one of the salespeople who could not attend with the group. Based on what I had learned, I emphasized the need to get down to basic needs. At first, we started out like the previous group: all the standard answers. When I challenged the salesperson, he insisted that these were the points he used to sell the product (and he was one of their top salespeople, by the way). Like the child that keeps asking the adult, "Why?" I kept up my annoying ritual until we finally arrived at a fantastically revealing level. Once we peeled back the standard responses, he was able to provide amazingly keen insight into the psyche of their customers and what really made the company's products appealing to them.

I'm not sure whether it's because the concept of Shiny Objects Marketing is too simple, and people want to hold onto something more mysterious, or because it is sometimes simply difficult to look beyond the obvious. Either way, it can be a challenge to get people thinking about the shiny objects behind the features and benefits. The following chart shows the typical feature a company is likely to identify, the need it could fill, and the shiny object that personifies the need. Notice how the shiny object is much more alluring than the actual feature.

Feature	Need	Shiny Object
Lose five pounds a week	Social acceptance	Look great in a bikini
Double the output speed	Recognition	Get accolades from your boss
Microlift antiwrinkle cream	Social acceptance	Make your face irresistible
3-in-1 fitness machine	Self-esteem	Get the body you've always wanted
Provide a full seven hours of sleep	Sleep	Start enjoying life
Reduce cholesterol	Health	Be healthy enough to enjoy retirement

To illustrate the point further, here are a few examples of the standard feature/benefit-type responses I have received over the years and the ultimate shiny object we discovered.

FDIC Insured

We were working with a company that provided paycards to payroll departments as an alternative to hard checks. As we began creating a list of possible shiny objects, "FDIC Insured" popped up immediately. Not to be taken lightly, the fact that each card was individually FDIC insured was a major benefit, and the company insisted that this should be up toward the top of the list. However, as we discussed it, it became evident there was little likelihood that the average payroll manager woke up in the morning thinking, "Gosh, I really want to find cards that are FDIC insured today." It's hard to imagine this same person walking into his or her office, calling their staff together and stating, "Okay team, our number one goal today is to find a company that provides cards that are individually FDIC insured." There is no doubt that this is a huge selling point, but it is not a shiny object. The question is "Why is FDIC-insured a big deal?" The reasoning went something like this: "If the cards are FDIC insured, they'll be covered in the event that a catastrophe occurs at the bank. This will protect me personally from being taken down by a vendor. I want to minimize risk, not increase it. I want to make my job simpler, not more difficult." Bingo! There's the shiny object. It's not about being FDIC insured; it's about proving to the payroll manager that this product will make his or her job easier.

As a test, I always like to see if I can put the shiny object into the prospective buyer's average day. So, is it possible that a payroll manager could wake up in the morning thinking (especially after worrying all night about everything he or she needed to do the next day), "Gosh, I really need to find a way to make my job easier" or call his staff together and say, "Okay team, we need to simplify things around here"? A definite *yes* to both.

Personalized URL

We were developing a series of programs with a company that had been a traditional printer for years but was now attempting to expand its list of services, one of which was a system of personalized mailings. This system had a long list of features and benefits that held tremendous potential to the customers, who were primarily marketing and advertising executives. However, the company's salespeople had two problems: First—they weren't the first ones on the block offering the service, and second—the features in and of themselves did not convey a tremendous opportunity. They identified the personalized URL feature as the key point. This feature, in essence, allowed you to send a mailer to a prospective customer that prompted them to go to a web site that had their name in the web address. Once again, I asked that we test the idea by putting it into the prospective customer's average day. When they walked into the lobby of their office that day were they thinking, "Man, I need to find someone that provides personalized URLs"? Probably not. Marketing and advertising executives are always in a tenuous situation. I know, because I've been one my entire career. You are only as good as your last program, and you are always one step away from being blamed for the entire company's failure. (Okay, I'm dramatizing it a bit, but it is very true that marketing and advertising budgets are the first to go in a downturn.) It is evident to anyone who has ever been in this industry that job security is a great big shiny object. So, was there a way to link personalized URLs to job security? Yes, indeed. First of all, we realized that claiming a direct mail program could provide job security was a little too much for an advertising executive to swallow. However, we felt confident that we could lay out a convincing case for the number one factor that improves job security—increased profits. Figure 5.1 is the chart we developed for the company that illustrated the pathway to the shiny object.

Heavy Duty

Several years ago, we developed an ad campaign for the introduction of a new type of digital multimeter. Like other multimeters before

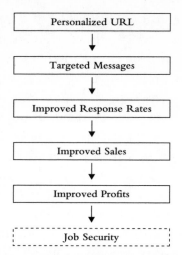

Figure 5.1   PURL Shiny Object Chart

it, it measured amps, volts, and ohms and gave the readout in digital numbers. Unlike the other meters, the company described this one as "heavy duty." Today, there are a great many heavy-duty voltmeters; but at that time, all other digital multimeters were somewhat fragile. This instrument, in contrast, was designed to be used by electricians outdoors in the worst kind of conditions and could take a lot of abuse. However, even though it was truly the first heavy duty digital multimeter, the term "heavy duty" was tremendously overused in the electrical industry. It almost seemed that everything was heavy duty. So the key feature of the product—the one that had the potential of making the product extremely successful—also had the possibility of being invisible because of the term used to describe it. A true dilemma.

Our creative team had the good sense to ask, "Is it really 'heavy duty' that people want? Or is there something simpler, more basic?" And they asked the right people—electricians. They heard horror story after horror story about myriad ways these guys destroyed multimeters. Ultimately, the team came up with one of the best lines I've ever seen in advertising. It was, in one breath, the shiny object, and a great headline. It simply read, "Oops Proof."

6 | Shiny Object Quadrants

The previous chapters defined what a shiny object is and how it can affect both your life and your brand. At this point, we are going to put all that information to work and discuss how to determine which attributes of your brand, product, or service make it a shiny object.

The key notion to keep in mind is that we are searching for your customer's shiny object—not *yours*. In all my years of advertising and marketing, this is the single hardest concept to grasp. Far too many marketing executives see everything through the prism of their companies and their products, and it becomes extremely difficult for them to step out of their roles and view their companies as outsiders do. The trouble that execs have putting themselves in their customers' shoes is one of the primary reasons that marketing and advertising agencies exist. These agencies exist outside of the culture and day-to-day perceptions of the clients—and the agencies ask the dumb questions that often lead to revelations.

My very first job in advertising was in the marketing communications department of a large electronics firm named Beckman Instruments in Southern California. I was so wet behind the ears that I believed everything that everyone said. I would go to a focus group or read a readership study and be confounded by the contradictions between what our customers said they wanted and what actually worked. My boss, Dan Rime, taught me three extremely valuable principles that I will never forget. They have been guiding stars for my entire professional life.

The first principle was: *It doesn't matter what people say they want to hear. It only matters what actually motivates them to buy.* People—especially the ones in focus groups—will tell you what they think you want to hear or what they think they should say. That's not to say that focus groups can't be very useful, but it is extremely difficult to get participants to express their true feelings. The closest I ever came to extracting real information from people in a focus group was by putting all of the participants under hypnosis. But short of that, people can't be completely trusted to tell you what really motivates them. The fact is,

77

most of the time, they don't really know what motivates them in the first place. They act on impulses or primal needs. Why does a person buy a four-wheel drive SUV to drive around town, never intending to take it into the snow or off-road? Why does someone buy professional cooking equipment at home when they usually eat out? Why does someone insist on buying a house with a pool that they never dip a foot in?

People are full of contradictions. The only true measure of what motivates your customers to buy is their actions. *Actions usually don't lie.* People don't spend their hard-earned cash on a product just to convince a researcher that they want the product. They buy it because they really want it—even if only for that moment. They are compelled to purchase because the product is their shiny object.

The second principle I learned was: *Don't trust what people in the company say the customer wants. Listen to what they say. Test it. But if it doesn't work, don't be surprised. The only one who matters is the customer.* Far too many executives in companies—whether they are presidents, engineers, marketing executives, or salespeople—have inflexible blinders on when it comes to their own products. They see them, as they want to see them or need to see them. Sometimes it's because they have invested millions of dollars in the development of a product and are too caught up in it to admit that it is a failure. Sometimes the whole project was their idea, and they can't afford to lose face. Sometimes they have too much blind faith in their research to accept that it may be wrong. Or maybe it's a simple case of "We've always sold it that way."

Whatever the reason, I have come up against countless executives who have real problems seeing the product from the customer's point of view. These managers need to be constantly reminded that the shiny object we're looking for belongs to the customer, not the company.

One of the best examples of the catastrophic results of looking at the shiny object from your own instead of the consumer's perspective is the dismal failure of the U.S. government's anti-drug campaign.

In 2006, the U.S. Government Accountability Office (U.S. GAO) issued a report that stated the anti-drug campaign that the government had been running for over eight years was ineffective. According to the study, after spending $1.2 billion on radio and TV, the ads did not have any measurable effect on reducing drug use. The first campaign had attempted to appeal to both parents and teens, and positioned them as "the anti-drug." The subsequent campaign went directly to the youth and encouraged them to be "above the influence" instead of under the influence (U.S. GAO 2006, 5).

The results of the $43 million, government-funded study by Westat Inc. and the University of Pennsylvania found that parents and youths remembered the ads and their messages. But the study also uncovered the fact that exposure to the ads did not change kids' attitudes about drugs because they did not relate to the ad messages. The ads did not appeal to the youths' shiny object. What kid is going to determine that he or she is the anti-drug? And what is it about being "above the influence" that is going to relate to a teenager? To make matters worse, the same study found the ad campaign might have actually *increased* drug use. The Westat study said that the teens could interpret the ads to suggest that marijuana use is more common and socially acceptable than it actually is. Boy, that's $1.4 billion well spent (U.S. GAO 2006, 42).

And how did the government's drug czar, John Walters, react to such devastating news? He asked Congress for $120 million more for the campaign—a $20 million increase from the prior year. You have to admire that kind of blind dogged persistence. Shiny object, be damned! Full speed ahead!

The third and final lesson I learned at the beginning of my career was: *It doesn't matter what you think about the ad. It doesn't matter what I think about the ad. It doesn't even really matter what the customer thinks about the ad. The only thing that matters is what the customer does after seeing the ad.* I have been astounded in creative presentation meetings where the client has objected to the concept based on his or her own personal biases. Case in point: I had a client shoot down a perfectly good idea once because the ad had an elephant in it, and the client didn't like elephants. I wondered what his personal distaste for pachyderms could have to do with selling his product to customers! The answer was nothing. Absolutely nothing. Because that client saw everything through the prism of his own experiences, he could not understand how an elephant might actually be appealing to someone, given the right situation.

Another instance of this was a postcard campaign my agency presented that focused on the needs of the client's customers, rather than on the client. Prior to this, the ads had always shown suit-bedecked salespeople shaking the proverbial hand of the customer. Instead of following this established approach, the new campaign focused on the real issues of the customers—real shiny objects. Several people inside the company objected to the campaign because it did not show a single person wearing a suit or tie. They were convinced that their storeowners would not feel the ads portrayed them properly. Heck! Our point had nothing to do with how we portrayed them at all. Fortunately, the president of the company caught the vision of the shiny object, stepped in, and righted the floundering discussion before the concept completely capsized. He invoked that principle that I had learned many years before: *It doesn't matter what you think about the ad. It doesn't matter what I think about the ad. It doesn't even really matter what the customer thinks about the ad. The only thing that matters is what the customer does after seeing the ad.*

Building the Quadrants

Through the years, I developed a tool called the *shiny object quadrants* that focuses only on those shiny objects that will produce the desired results. The intent of this tool is to provide a technique for people to back away from their own preconceived notions and allow the shiny objects to rise to the surface.

At AdMatrix, we conduct hands-on seminars called "Shiny Object Workshops" in which we show people how to put these quadrants to use in their companies. Over the next several pages, I am going to share these quadrants with you and show you how to interpret them. Though this process takes some effort to accomplish, the result is often a dramatic insight about what really attracts your customers. So, hang in there.

These shiny object quadrants are formed by two intersecting axes (shown in Figures 6.1 and 6.2): the *desire to have* and the *ability to provide*.

Desire to Have

This metric is measured entirely from the customer's perspective. This is a ranking of all the possible shiny objects your customer might want, according to their desire to have. Money does not come into play here. I am not talking about actually putting down cash to be able to grab the shiny object. It simply encompasses the raw desire to possess it.

Ability to Provide

This metric is measured entirely from your *company's* perspective. This is a ranking of your ability to provide the shiny objects that your

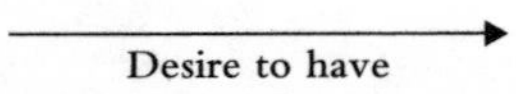

Desire to have ⟶

Figure 6.1   Desire-to-Have Axis

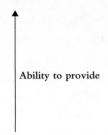

Figure 6.2   Ability-to-Provide Axis

customers want. Again, notice that there is no mention of money. Whether you can make money selling the shiny object has no bearing at this point. This is simply your ability to create and deliver the shiny object.

The intersection of these two axes forms four quadrants, which are detailed in Figure 6.3.

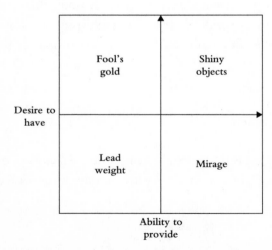

Figure 6.3   Shiny Objects Quadrants

Lower Left: Lead Weight—Low Desire to Have/Low Ability to Provide

Nobody wants it, and you have a hard time providing it. It may seem crazy, but there are many companies that have products and services that fall into this quadrant. It might be that the product was at one time in demand or that the ability to provide the product has changed based on government regulations or scarcity of raw materials. Whatever the case, if you have products in this category, get rid of them. They are dragging the company down.

Several years ago, I worked for an advertising agency that had a security company as a client. This company produced a wide range of products used to foil counterfeiters, one of which was a prism tape that had three-dimensional codes laser etched into it. It was virtually impossible to duplicate without millions of dollars worth of equipment. However, that also meant that the company needed millions of dollars worth of equipment to produce it. This resulted in a hefty price tag for the tape, making it noncompetitive with other technologies. Regardless of the superior performance of the product, the company could not get anyone to step up and buy it. Despite the fact that the product was extremely difficult to produce and no one apparently wanted it, the company (against our advice) continued to pursue a hefty marketing campaign. Eventually, financially and emotionally exhausted, the company dropped the product from its lineup.

Upper Left: Fool's Gold—Low Desire to Have/High Ability to Provide

It looks like the real thing, but it's worthless. This quadrant is characterized by products that are sitting on the shelf with little to no chance of getting sold. There are countless instances where companies have put millions of dollars into producing something that no one wants. They are absolutely convinced that "if they build it, they will come." Products in this category are hard to let go. Often, they either work fantastically or there is an emotional attachment that blinds the upper echelons to the fact that the product simply won't sell. Companies caught by the gleam of *fool's gold* often continue to pour millions into marketing, convinced that the market will eventually see the light and come around to their way of thinking.

A great example of a company that was mining for fool's gold was Sony, when it kept chasing the Betamax video format long after the market abandoned it. Sony introduced Betamax in 1975, and it quickly gained success in the professional video market. Building on this early success, Sony made an attempt to establish itself as the industry standard and quickly gained contracts with many of the major home electronics manufacturers—including Toshiba, Pioneer, Aiwa, NEC, and Zenith—to produce VCRs based on the Betamax format. It certainly looked like Sony was set to be the international video giant—except there was one holdout. JVC declined an offer by Sony to join the fray and, instead, decided to develop its own technology. In 1976, JVC introduced the Video Home System, better known as VHS. They made the tactical decision to make the format lower quality—and hence, less expensive—than Betamax but to beef it up with a host of nifty features that Betamax did not offer. For example VHS's construction made it able to rewind and fast-forward much faster than Betamax (Wielage and Woodcock 1988).

The tactic worked. People flocked to the cheaper units, mesmerized by all the bells and whistles. By 1980—only four years later— JVC owned 70 percent of the North American market. Sony clung onto its format for years, insisting that it was a superior technology and that consumers would eventually come around. By 1984, 40 companies utilized the VHS format—in comparison with Beta's 12. Finally, in 1988, with less than 2.5 percent of the market, Sony finally threw in the towel and started manufacturing its own VHS recorders (Wielage and Woodcock 1988).

The fact of matter was that Betamax truly was a superior technology. From the cassette's mechanism to the tracking system, Betamax outperformed VHS every time. But people simply didn't care. It was too pricey and didn't have all the goodies that VHS came with. So Betamax remained fool's gold.

Lower Right: Mirage—High Desire to Have/Low Ability to Provide

You can see it in the distance, but you can never reach it. This is a very common quadrant for many companies to find themselves in. They identify a viable market and attempt to create a product to sell into it. However, despite their best efforts, they simply can't seem to provide what the market demands. It might be because they can't produce anything that meets the customer's expectations; or maybe they aren't able figure out how to distribute the product efficiently; or perhaps they simply aren't capable of getting a fix on exactly who the market is. Whatever the reason, this product is their *mirage*. The closer you get to it, the farther away it seems to move—and then it evaporates altogether.

Marketing books are full of examples of companies chasing mirages. One of these is the case of Everett Charles, a company that, back in 1975, decided to build a robotic electronics assembler. The company spent a fortune on research and determined there was an enormous market for such a product. They even had presales by companies that were standing in line to buy the system. Clearly, the cost of R&D was grossly overshadowed by the potential return. The central core of this invention was a robotic arm that was delicate enough to pick up an egg, yet strong enough to pick up lead weights (personal communication with Kenneth Church, February 15, 2008).

Everett Charles sunk millions of dollars into producing the system; but each time they got close to their goal, a new problem would arise, and they would have to spend another million to fix it. At one point, General Electric (GE) came for a demonstration of the machine delicately soldering and assembling the tympanic membrane of a telephone. GE was so impressed that they were practically ready to pay in cash. However, there were still too many bugs to work out, and the assembler was not quite ready to sell. By the time Everett Charles had worked out the bugs, the price had escalated beyond what GE could afford. Eventually, the company realized that the only organization that would be able to stomach the staggering price tag would be a government. So, Everett Charles went to demonstrate their mechanical marvel at a robotics trade show in Peking, China. To their delight, it was a huge success—the hit of the show. Only one problem . . . when it came time to leave, the Chinese government wouldn't let Everett Charles take their prototype (their only prototype). It seems that there was a law in China at that time that any electronic devices brought into the country had to stay. Despite their appeals to the government, the robot stayed. The cost to rebuild a prototype from scratch was simply more than they could bear and they finally gave up.

The phrase "throwing good money after bad" comes to mind. Companies that find themselves in these situations might abide by the advice of W. C. Fields (n.d.) who said, "If at first you don't succeed, try again. Then quit. No use being a damn fool about it" (Fields n.d.).

Psychologists, of course, have a term for the behavior exhibited by companies like Everett Charles. They call it *irrational escalation of commitment* (IEC), which refers to people who make irrational decisions to justify actions already taken. This is a downward spiral that can take a company all the way to ruin. Certainly, there have been many products that have been destroyed by this type of decision making. Products and services in the mirage quadrant need to be carefully evaluated. Otherwise, companies can find themselves investing millions of dollars only to find nothing to show for it.

One of the best examples of this was the EV1 produced by General Motors (GM). At first appearance, the market for this product seemed to be perfect. In 1990, California had more vehicles on the road than any other state. In an attempt to control the air pollution caused by these millions of cars, the State of California issued the Zero Emissions Vehicle (ZEV) mandate which stated that by 1998, two percent of all new cars sold by the seven major auto manufacturers in the state of California were to meet "zero emission" standards as defined by the California Air Resources Board (CARB). This number would go up to 10 percent by 2003 (Moore 2003).

GM introduced EV1s in 1997 based on a prototype electric vehicle called the *Impact*. Only 600 of these cars hit the road that year, and they were available only as a lease. The car was a technological marvel. It was designed and built from the bottom up as an electric vehicle and not a conversion, as many of the competitors were. It had a fraction of the moving parts that a combustible engine had and required virtually no maintenance. It was the most aerodynamic vehicle in history and could accelerate from 0 to 60 in eight seconds. It was immediately praised by drivers and auto magazines and was touted as the future of the auto industry (U.S. Department of Education 1999).

However, the EV1 enjoyed a short period of success, and the cause of the car's untimely demise lay in the batteries. GM banked on the belief that by the time people started to accept the EV1 in large numbers, battery technology would have evolved to the point that the car would be practical. However, that hope was never fulfilled. One of the reasons that people had to lease the car and couldn't buy it was because the lead-acid—and the later nickel metal

hydride—batteries wore out after a few years and had to be replaced
to the tune of thousands of dollars. At its best, the EV1 could only
get between 75 to 100 miles on a charge, and a full recharge took
as long as eight hours. If you got stuck on the road with your batteries dead, there weren't many places to get a charge. Edison provided several charging stations around Southern California, but they
were few and far between. Another problem with the battery technology was that the batteries could not hold a consistent charge in
cold weather—which meant the cars were unsuitable for most of
the country (Adams 2001).

But GM didn't give up quickly on this mirage. By the time the
EV1 program died, GM had spent over $1 billion developing and
marketing the EV1. Despite the battery problems, they persevered.

The death knell for the EV1 came in 2001. The CARB changed
the ZEV mandate to allow manufacturers to claim partial ZEV
credit for hybrid vehicles—which were much simpler to manufacture and were more practical when it came to driving distances. By
2003, CARB removed the requirement for total electric vehicles
from the ZEV mandate. GM suddenly found itself with a car that
had no market. At this point, they had no choice but to cancel the
program and let the mirage fade away.

Upper Right: Shiny Objects—High Desire to Have/High Ability to Provide

The sweet spot—where people want what you can provide. This is
the win-win quadrant. The customers get what they want, and you
make money by providing it. It seems simple enough; but very few
companies actually end up in this quadrant for an extended length of
time. Sometimes they wander in by accident. Other times, they get
there purposefully but without understanding truly where they are,
or why they are successful. Those that do have shiny objects rarely

reach the upper right corner of this quadrant—where the customer absolutely demands what you provide, and it is brain-dead easy to provide. Plus, if you are fortunate enough to obtain this nirvana, there are usually hordes of competitors that suddenly show up to mimic your efforts.

Now that you understand the basic nature of the shiny objects quadrants, its time to see where your customers' shiny objects fall.

Step One: List Your Customers' Shiny Objects

The first step to discovering which quadrant your customers' shiny objects fall into is to create a comprehensive list of their shiny objects as they relate to your product, service, or brand. Your customers have many shiny objects in their lives. Some will connect with your product or service. Most will not. It is essential, however, that you thoroughly explore all aspects of your product that might be related to their shiny objects.

This is the most important step in setting up the shiny object quadrants. It is extremely critical to get every shiny object possible out on the table or up on the whiteboard. There is often a hidden gem that the marketing department overlooks. The point of this exercise is to consider the various aspects of your product from your customer's point of view. Something that you consider insignificant might turn out to be hugely important to your customers. So, don't worry about how long the list might be. At our Shiny Objects Workshops we often start with a list of over 50 shiny objects. You can always pare them down. But if a shiny object is not brought out into the open, you won't have the chance to even evaluate it.

In the Shiny Object Workshops, we take a stab at this step by brainstorming all the possible shiny objects; however, this step is so important that I usually suggest to my clients that they conduct formal research to get into the heads of the customer and have them identify their own shiny objects. All too often, we assume that we know our customers inside and out. We sit in a room and make a list of what we think attracts our customers. While this isolation is sometimes unavoidable because there aren't enough funds to pay for research, it is very dangerous to hang the future of your product on what the *provider* thinks the customers' shiny objects are. As I mentioned before, research is not perfect; and many times, people aren't exactly truthful in what they say. But there are many types of research that can evaluate what people do (as opposed to what they say) when confronted with various shiny objects. Plus, any research is better than guessing.

The following chart offers a short list of shiny objects as an example. There are two ways to develop this list. First, you identify all the features of your product and how they translate to benefits, needs, and ultimately: shiny objects. But sometimes you might miss something that is critical to the customer by initiating the process by listing these features. So it is equally important to work the process in the opposite direction. Identify any shiny object that is not on the list, and then determine the need from which it springs, the benefit that relates to that need, and finally, any features on which the benefit is based. By following this procedure, you will identify a comprehensive list of shiny objects.

Feature	Benefit	Need	Shiny Object
Account manager assigned to your account	We make every step simple to complete	Physiological	Easy
We manage the whole program	You can focus on more important issues	Self-actualization	More time
Services all have successful track records	No risk to try these services	Safety	Job security

Feature	Benefit	Need	Shiny Object
In-house consultants help you design your program	Every program is designed to be successful	Self actualization	Ideas that sell the product
Full reporting functions	Reports provide visibility of your successful program	Esteem	Recognition
Integrated services reduce overall cost	Any size company can utilize this program	Safety	Compete with the big guys
All programs developed by a nationally known sales guru	Proven programs to grow your business	Safety	Expand my business
Very active user base from over 100 companies	Connect with people that share your same issues	Social	Be part of a successful trend
We handle the details	No need to worry about the details	Physiological	Reduce stress

Step Two: Determine the Relevance of the Factors That Effect Desire to Have and Ability to Provide

To plot your customers' shiny objects, you need to assign a numerical value to each one. I developed a system that creates an affinity rating of each shiny object based on how much it relates to a standard set of factors. These factors never change from product to product, service to service, or brand to brand. If they don't relate to the shiny object at all, they are assigned a value of 0. If they relate to the shiny object 100 percent, they get a 2. If they relate somewhat, but they sort of don't, give it a 1. Then you simply add up the score of the factors.

Factors That Determine the Desire to Have

We use the Shiny Object Workshop to create a consensus session to rate these factors. This is much more effective and more reliable than simply doing it by yourself; but once again, I highly recommend conducting research to score these factors. Otherwise, we are simply guessing about what our customers think is important:

- *Critical to sustaining life:* This means exactly what it says. You need to ask yourself if your customers can live without this shiny object or if they will literally die without it. In the previous chart, let's evaluate the shiny object "job security" as an example. Is it critical to sustaining life? Well, if you don't have a job, you can't buy food, and food is pretty essential to living. However, a lot people get along pretty well with jobs that aren't very secure. So, let's give it a score of 1. It relates somewhat.

- *Vital to my protection:* According to Maslow's Needs Hierarchy, *protection* refers to protecting family, friends, work, market share . . . and so on. It also relates to safety and security. Again let's look at the shiny object "job security." By definition, job security is a protection, so we'll give a 2; relates to the shiny object 100 percent.

- *Important to my being accepted:* This could refer to acceptance at work, at home, in the community, or among friends. Using the job security example, how does being accepted relate? Not at all. So, we'll give a 0.

- *Crucial for my self-esteem:* This includes confidence, achievement, and respect of and by others. Job security in this case could make you feel better about yourself but, once again, there are many people with insecure jobs that have excellent self-esteem. So, let's give it a 1.

- *Important to make life rewarding:* At the apex of Maslow's Needs is self-actualization, which includes creativity, spontaneity, and problem solving. Finally what does this have to do with job security? I think most people would agree that if they had a job for life, assuming it's a job they want and like, life would be very rewarding. This definitely deserves a 2.

Figure 6.4 illustrates how the desire-to-have factors might look using the shiny object examples listed previously.

Shiny Objects	Critical to sustaining life	Vital to my protection	Important to my being accepted	Crucial for my self-esteem	Important to make life rewarding	Total
Easy	0	0	0	0	2	2
More time	0	0	0	0	2	2
Job security	1	2	0	1	2	6
Ideas	0	1	2	2	1	6
Recognition	0	2	2	2	2	8
Compete with the *big guys*	0	1	1	2	1	5
Expand	0	2	2	2	1	7
Trust	0	0	2	2	2	6
Reduce stress	1	1	0	0	2	4

Figure 6.4 Desire-to-Have Chart

Factors That Determine the Ability to Provide

Unlike the factors that determine the desire to have, these factors are solely determined by you and your company and don't typically require research. However, if you have an especially complex organization with multiple layers, it may be very possible that you are insulated from reality. In that case, an internal research project might uncover perspectives of which you were completely unaware. It's always better to know what is actually going on rather than being blindsided. Consider the following issues and aspects of your shiny object:

- *Direct result of your product:* Does the natural by-product or net effect of your product/service result in the shiny object?
- *Availability of resources (people, raw materials, equipment):* Do you have the wherewithal to actually produce the feature that results in the shiny object?
- *Actively help customer:* Do you get in the trenches with your customer and make the effort to help them attain the shiny object?
- *No effort to provide:* Even if you can produce the feature that results in the shiny object, is it incredibly easy to do so?
- *Repeatable and consistent:* Can you continue to provide the shiny object over and over again?

Figure 6.5 illustrates how the ability-to-provide factors might look using the shiny object examples listed previously.

Step Three: Plot the Shiny Objects into the Quadrants

All you need to do now is plot desire to have and ability to provide on the shiny object quadrants. Using the previous examples, the chart would look like Figure 6.6.

Shiny Objects	Direct result of your product	Availability of resources	Actively help customer	No effort to provide	Repeatable and consistent	Total
Easy	2	1	1	0	1	5
More time	2	0	1	1	2	6
Job security	1	0	1	0	0	2
Ideas	2	2	2	2	1	9
Recognition	2	1	1	2	1	7
Compete with the *big guys*	2	2	2	1	2	9
Expand	2	2	2	2	1	9
Trust	2	1	1	1	0	5
Reduce stress	1	1	0	1	0	3

Figure 6.5   Ability-to-Provide Chart

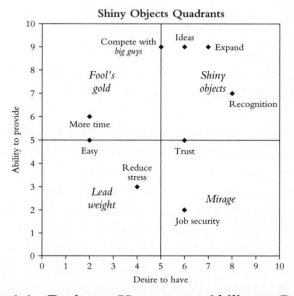

Figure 6.6   Desire to Have versus Ability to Provide

This rendition of the shiny objects quadrants tells us the following:

- *Lead weight:* Don't even think about promoting the fact that your product can reduce stress. Although it might seem like a great idea to the guys down in the advertising department, our analysis shows that this is most likely a loser.
- *Mirage:* Although it might be tempting because there seems to be a demand for job security, don't go there. No matter how bad people want it, you can't provide it.
- *Fool's gold*: Here's the hard one. According to this analysis, you are really good at making the program easy and providing more time. Who doesn't want more time and for things to be easy? Evidently, your customers. Both are very low on the desire-to-have scale.
- *Shiny objects*—Good news: you have three shiny objects squarely in the shiny objects quadrant—the top three are expanding the business, ideas, and recognition. According to this analysis, these look like winners. However, *we are not quite finished*. Read on!

Step Four: Add Money to the Equation and Replot Your Customers' Top Shiny Objects

The prior analysis was based solely on your customers' desires to have their shiny objects and your ability to provide them—without regard to any financial aspects. It was designed to analyze the shiny objects, only considering them on their own merits. At this point, we need to identify the shiny objects that can be profitable; so we add money to equation. After all, you can only build a profit base around shiny objects that motivate people to part with their money.

Rather than apply this metric to all the shiny objects, we are only interested in those that fall into the shiny object quadrant. This provides a process to refine the shiny objects into the shiniest of the shiny. Once again, if the specific factor doesn't relate to the shiny object at all, it is assigned a value of 0. If it relates to the shiny object 100 percent, it gets a 2. If it relates sometimes or only a little, then give it a 1. Then simply add the scores of the factors.

Factors That Determine Desire to Buy

People will often take whatever you offer—if it's free. However, if they have to pull out their wallets, they suddenly become more discriminating. It's not unusual for a top-rated desire-to-have shiny object to drop to the bottom of the chart as soon as you put a price on it. These factors are designed to sift the chaff from the wheat and help you keep only those shiny objects that have the power to produce a sale:

- *Willingness to pay:* It is not enough for your customers to simply want the shiny object. Do your customers desire it enough to put down cash to possess it?
- *Top budget item:* If they are willing to pay money to purchase the shiny object, is it a top priority? Will they put it ahead of their purchase of other shiny objects?
- *Confidence that it can be provided*: Okay, we know they want it, but do they have confidence that someone out there can provide it?
- *Urgency to purchase:* Do your customers want the shiny object so badly that they are willing to hand over their money right now?
- *Willingness to go into debt to obtain*: Even if they don't have the money to buy the shiny object, do they desire it so strongly that they will borrow money to own it?

The shiny objects that fell into the shiny object quadrants described earlier were expand/grow, ideas/help, recognition/promotion/success,

Shiny Objects	Willingness to pay	Top budget item	Confidence that it can be provided	Urgency to purchase	Willingness to go into debt to obtain	Total
Expand/grow	2	2	1	2	2	9
Ideas/help	1	0	2	1	0	4
Recognition/promotion/success	0	0	0	0	0	0
Compete with the *big guys*	2	2	1	2	1	8
Trust/comfort/confidence	0	0	2	0	0	2

Figure 6.7   Desire-to-Buy Chart

compete with the big guys, and trust/comfort/confidence. Combining these shiny objects with the factors in the list could produce a chart that looks like Figure 6.7.

Factors That Determine Ability to Sell

Just being able to provide a shiny object does not mean that you will be able to sell it. Once you put a price tag on it, the rules change. These factors are designed to pinpoint the shiny objects that will move off the shelf:

- *Ability to relate product to shiny object:* Can your sales and marketing department translate the features and benefits of your product into shiny objects that your customers can understand?

- *No internal training required:* Are the people in your sales and marketing channel so up-to-date on the product and your customer base that they do not need any special training?
- *All customers can afford it:* Not a few, not some, not many, and not even most. Can *all* of your customers afford your product?
- *Available and shiny:* You can't sell your product if is not available when the object becomes shiny. This is particularly important for seasonal products and services. Are you ready to go the moment your customers desire the shiny object?
- *Ability to communicate to customer:* You need to be able to locate and talk to your customers if you expect to sell them anything. Do you have the funds and skills to find your customers and communicate with them?

Utilizing these shiny object factors could produce a chart that looks like Figure 6.8.

Shiny Objects	Ability to relate product to shiny object	No internal training required	All customers can afford it	Available and shiny	Ability to communicate to customer	Total
Expand/grow	2	1	1	2	2	8
Ideas/help	2	2	2	2	1	9
Recognition/promotion/success	1	0	2	0	0	3
Compete with the *big guys*	2	1	1	2	2	8
Trust/comfort/confidence	1	2	2	2	0	7

Figure 6.8   Ability-to-Sell Chart

As our final step, we plot these factors on the shiny object quadrants as before, which gives us the information in Figure 6.9.

Notice the significant shift once money entered the equation. In Figure 6.6, expand, ideas, and recognition were all highly rated shiny objects. Now, in Figure 6.9 with money in the picture, ideas and trust have shifted to fool's gold while recognition dropped down to lead weight. Compete with the big guys shot into shiny objects, and expand rose to the very top. Based on this analysis, compete with the big guys and expand are the two strongest shiny objects to attract customers.

Congratulations. You have just discovered the aspects of your product or service that will make it a shiny object to your customers. As such, it will fulfill a primal need. It is not necessary for you to

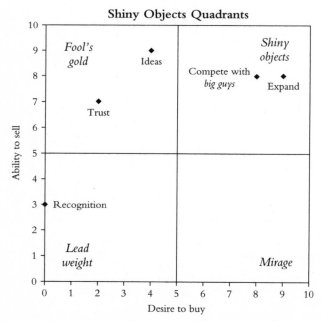

Figure 6.9   Desire to Buy versus Ability to Sell

create a lengthy, persuasive narrative to convince your customers to pay attention. They will do it naturally. Remember, every shiny object relates to a basic need. In the previous case, "expand the business" related to safety.

Don't be lulled into thinking that now that you have discovered the shiny object, all you have to do is hang it up and people will flock to you. To be a true shiny object, it must conform to the *five facets* of shiny objects. To discover these facets and how to make sure your shiny objects comply with them, read on.

7 | Five Facets of Shiny Objects

To be truly powerful, a shiny object must do more than just catch your prospects' eye. It must take them through a process that ultimately results with an overwhelming *urge* to possess it.

Remember the raccoon? Once he sees the shiny object, he isn't content to simply gaze at it. Instead, the shiny object has such power over him that he has to grab it and not let go. How would you like your customers to be like that? They certainly will be, if you make sure that your customers' shiny objects contain all five facets described later.

Sometimes these shiny object facets could appear to happen very quickly or even simultaneously; however, every shiny object must attain each facet to truly be a shiny object. The facets occur in a precise order:

Five Facets of Shiny Objects
1. Grabs your attention
2. Creates a driving curiosity
3. Stimulates an irrepressible urge to touch
4. Activates an emotion
5. Demands ownership

1. Grabs Your Attention

This is probably the most obvious of the shiny object facets because it is the one of which people are most aware. It is definitely the first effect that a shiny object has on us; after all, we initially become aware of a shiny object because it catches our eye. However, for the purposes of marketing a product, service, or brand, we are not merely concerned about creating a casual distraction. In fact, the operative question for this facet is, "What will cause your customers to stop dead in their tracks and take notice of what you are selling?"

This is a universal question as it relates to shiny objects—whether you are selling car parts, software, financial services, or even yourself. Imagine going on a job interview. You not only want your prospective boss to notice that you stand out in the crowd, but you also want your presence to actually *grab* his attention. This can be accomplished based on the combination of how you look and what you say; and this is true no matter what you're selling. If you don't fully capture your prospects' interest, and make them stop for a moment to pay attention, your efforts will be fruitless.

I typically use the example of a trade show exhibit to help people understand the five shiny object facets. For a trade show exhibit to successfully market your customer's shiny object, it must possess all five of these characteristics. Consider the first facet, and visualize a potential customer walking down the aisles of a trade show where there are hundreds, maybe thousands, of exhibits. All of them are creating visual noise—so much noise, in fact, that they all begin to blend into one big cacophony. In the midst of this bedlam, prospects begin to approach your exhibit. You only have one chance to literally stop them dead in their tracks and compel them to take notice of you. If you can't accomplish this, they will keep walking, and you will miss the chance to give them your sales pitch.

Although I use this trade show example to convey how urgent it is to gain a potential client's attention, this situation exists every time someone opens a magazine, drives down the road, reads e-mail, surfs the web, or turns on the television. The mediums change but the principle remains the same: You only have a *split second* to make someone pause momentarily and thus secure that person's attention.

So, how do you make sure your shiny object is grabbing attention?

It Has to Be Shiny

This may seem obvious; but it is amazing how many companies simply don't understand this concept. People reach for the brass ring because it's shiny. If it's dull or uninteresting, they are not likely to reach for it.

Let's define *shiny* for a moment. Synonyms for *shiny* include glossy, gleaming, sparkly, glittery, polished, shimmering, glistening, and burnished. These are adjectives that describe something that is very appealing to the eye—something that is pleasing and beautiful. While it is true that you can grab someone's attention with something that is ugly and disgusting, it is unwise to leave that type of image associated with your product, unless there is a very strong strategic reason to do so. In the classic movie *The Hucksters* (Conway 1947), Clark Gable plays a disillusioned advertising man named Vic Norman who is confronted by the boorish owner of Beautee Soap, Mr. Evans. In an attempt to convince Norman that he needs to come up with a memorable ad campaign for his soap, Evans unexpectedly spits on his highly polished conference table. "Gentlemen," he growls, "You have just seen me do a disgusting thing. But you will always remember it!" And indeed I did. I saw that film over 20 years ago, and I still remember it. However, that kind of gratuitous negative image does not leave a lasting positive impression about your product or brand—and rarely will it be a shiny object to your customers.

Quite a bit has been written on the topic of "shock" advertising. If your audience is attracted to that type of shiny object, it might be worth looking into. However, for the majority of people, it's wise to consider how to present your shiny object in its best possible light. This includes excellent design, well-written copy, and attractive images. This is not to say that every ad or brochure you create should be a work of art; but it should definitely employ well-accepted rules of good design. This requires getting someone who is skilled in this particular area to create the material for you; and unfortunately, your cousin Bob or the wife of your sales manager will rarely possess the proficiency necessary to create good design. Just as you wouldn't dream of having your plumber represent you in court, you shouldn't put the future of your product in the hands of someone who is not a capable professional. There are hundreds of qualified graphic artists and ad agencies scraping for work that would love to take on your project.

Over the years, many great ideas have been killed by lackluster design. Many marketing and advertising directors who try to save money by skimping on design end up letting their shiny object become dull and unappealing, which results in mediocre sales. What is the point of saving money if it ends up costing you money? It is important as well to keep in mind that great design is not just made up of pretty pictures on a page. A professional designer methodically studies the message you are trying to convey and knows exactly how to lead your eye through the ad—right from the key message to the call to action. It's more about selling than it is about art.

The words you use to describe your shiny object are just as important as the manner in which you display it. Words have the power to convince and motivate. History is replete with great orators who have moved people to amazing action simply by the power and dynamics of the words they use. Many times—especially if your product is a service—the only way to convey your shiny object is through words. To this end, I often run my clients through an exercise where we identify the key descriptors of the shiny object. In this exercise, we start by brainstorming every word that comes to mind that relates to the shiny object. Then we start paring them down until we have the top five. This process typically produces very potent words that literally light up the shiny object.

It Must Be Shined from Time to Time

Once you have a great design coupled with powerful words, don't be lulled into the security that your work is done. All shiny objects, if left on their own for a period of time, will become dull. You need to pay constant attention to keep things polished and shiny.

My agency created a summer sale for one of our clients that produced results that went significantly beyond anyone's expectations. When it came time to run the sale the following year, the marketing manager decided to save some money by using the exact same materials we produced the year before. Not one item was changed. The result was predictably disappointing. Not only was the shiny object missing something new, but it had become dull over time. The market was saturated with the message from the year before and—although the message was still pertinent and the shiny object was still there, it looked like it was just a rehash of last year's idea. People were simply uninterested. They didn't stop in their tracks because they had seen it all before. The following year we produced an all-new campaign, still based on the same shiny object—but with all new images and materials. Not surprisingly, the results returned to the level of the first year. While I recognize that there were many factors in the market that could have influenced the return of positive results, none were as influential as the fact that the shiny object had been restored to its former brilliance.

It Has to Be in the Light

If your shiny object is in the dark, it can't shine. You can't grab attention with a shiny object that people can't see. To put your shiny object out where people can see it, you need to understand where your customers are, what their day-to-day habits include, and when they will have a chance to see your shiny object.

An example of failure to attain this feature: The International Kenpo Karate Association came to us with a problem. Their shiny object had been in the dark for so long that their brand had almost completely lost its equity. In 1954, a man by the name of Ed Parker developed a method of Karate that combined Kenpo and street fighting. He called it American Kenpo. In 1956, only two short years after creating this technique, it had become so popular that he founded the Kenpo Karate Association of America (KKAA), which in 1960 became the International Kenpo Karate Association (IKKA) and governed Kenpo and certify dojos (schools) and sensei (teachers) in the art, and provide structured competition throughout the world. Due to Mr. Parker's commitment, passion, and extensive travels, he converted thousands of martial artists to his technique. According to the IKKA, almost every practitioner and Kenpo organization can trace his or her roots back to Mr. Parker. At its height, the IKKA was one of the premier Karate organizations in the world. Unfortunately, Mr. Parker died in 1990, and the organization began to slowly decay. Other groups came onto the scene claiming to teach true Kenpo, and even the name IKKA was copied (Parker 1982, 34).

By the time the IKKA came to us, it was a shadow of its former greatness. However, it still had a strong foundation and many supporters around the world who continued to spread Mr. Parker's technique. Working in conjunction with the owners of the IKKA, we developed a strong campaign that focused on the theme, "We're back—Stronger than ever." The campaign focused on the tangible benefits that martial artists receive by being part of the IKKA. We even received endorsements by major dojos around the world.

The very nature of this campaign relied on the need to widely distribute the shiny object. It had to be seen everywhere that martial artists assembled. If you are trying to claim that you are "back," then you have to look like you're back. It would be counterproductive to make such a claim and then come back into the market with a whimper. No one can see your shiny object if you hang it in the dark.

But logic does not always prevail. The owners of the IKKA felt the best method to reintroduce the association back into the market would be through the dojos. They felt that by providing an incentive to dojos to convert their students to IKKA, they could rapidly regain their former greatness. Unfortunately, the sensei in the dojos were more interested in teaching than converting, and the incentive meant little to them. They were sensei because they loved to teach, not because they wanted to make money. They were happy to sign up anyone who asked, but without a widespread campaign, no one even knew that the IKKA had returned. Ultimately, the campaign died, and the IKKA has limped along ever since. You can't expect a shiny object to grab someone's attention if they can't see it.

Now, an example of success: We once had a client named Wyle Laboratories. When we started working for them, they were one of the top five distributors of electronic components in the United States. As with all distributors, Wyle did not manufacture anything. It simply resold products from major electronics manufacturers, and these same products were resold by a host of other distributors. Traditionally, distributors' primary competitive posture—other than price and delivery—was built around value-added services. These were services that enhanced the worth of the basic product by offering items such as special packaging, custom testing, and putting the components into kits. While interviewing the key executives of Wyle's value-added services, we came across a shiny object. It turns out that they were actually helping electronic engineers design customized semiconductors called Application Specific Integrated Circuits (ASICs). This service dramatically reduced the resources that companies had to invest to develop their own ASICs and also cut down on the time to market. Plus, Wyle turned out to be very good at this. Add the fact that no other distributor was offering this service and—Bingo! You've got one powerful shiny object.

It wasn't terribly difficult to convince Wyle that they should put this shiny object on a pedestal, but it was something different altogether to convince them to invest cash to promote it. They felt that, in time, people would become aware of the service. They had a few spec sheets and a very simple flier, but nothing that really touted the true benefits of the service. After several attempts, we convinced them to put some muscle behind this program and take it to the world. We created an entire campaign around this shiny object that included ads, articles, brochures, videos, direct mail, and even a design contest.

In less than two years, according to a study conducted by Electronic Engineering Times, Wyle moved from being perceived as just another distributor to the most technologically savvy distributor in the market. Whereas before engineers were very reluctant to discuss technical issues with a distributor (after all, all distributors do is sell parts), they were now calling Wyle on a regular basis for direction and recommendations regarding the semiconductors they sold. This encouraged other manufacturers of ASICs and other high-tech components to rely on Wyle to handle technical issues with engineers—which resulted in significantly higher sales (Engineers' Perception of Electronic Distributors 1991).

The results of this campaign surpassed everyone's greatest hopes and put Wyle into a superior position over its competitors—by putting the shiny object in the light.

It Has to Be Clear and Concise

Too many shiny objects on a page have the same effect as none at all: we simply don't respond. The term "information overload" was coined in 1970 by futurist Alvin Toffler in his book *Future Shock* (Toffler 1970, 350). The basic premise of this notion is that people have a difficult time processing multiple messages, and as they try to deal with more and more information, they either make the wrong decision or shut down altogether. This overload is caused by incessant interruptions. As you try to process one bit of information in an ad and are then confronted with another bit of information, you are interrupted from finalizing the first bit. Multiply this by eight or ten messages in an ad, and you have a meltdown. People will simply turn the page and forget everything they just saw.

A similar phenomenon is called "sensory overload." This term is often associated with autism, but is a common issue among the general population. It occurs when the senses are being deluged with input and the brain simply can't process it all. Although the brain is an amazing piece of machinery and is capable of processing multiple signals at the same time, it does have its limits. In a typical TV commercial, you are confronted with music, sound effects, song lyrics, words, a narrator, and images—all coming at you at blinding speed. If the TV spot is singularly focused on one shiny object, we can easily process all the information. But, if you are bombarded with more sensory information than you can handle, you become stressed and have an immediate desire to flee. Autistic people are particularly sensitive to sensory input and completely withdraw from reality to cope with the overload. The average person will merely tune out some or all of the input to manage the flow of information. Have you ever tried to have a conversation with someone who is intensely watching a movie? It's an almost impossible task. To process the information, we need to focus on one message at a time.

In the same way, an ad, brochure, web site, or any other form of communication that tries to say too much ends up saying nothing. The reader shuts down and moves on. This has been an ongoing challenge with clients throughout my career. They typically want to get the most out of their ads by trying to convey a long list of messages. White space seems like such a waste to them. But what they don't usually understand is that by hanging up multiple shiny objects, they create confusion and stress in the reader.

One of the best all time ads that focused on one, concise shiny object is the "Think Small" ad from Volkswagen. At the time the ad came out, U.S. auto manufacturers were still convinced that large cars were what Americans wanted. The ad from Volkswagen focused on the small size of their car and was designed to make it look especially tiny. The ad was almost entirely white space with a minute picture of the car in the upper-right corner. The headline was simply, "Think Small." The copy went on to extol the virtues of being small. It was one of the most successful ads of the twentieth century. Unfortunately, it's sad to say that most marketing directors I have met would have killed the ad by trying to improve it. And I am not alone in this supposition. In 1963, Fred Manley, vice president and creative director of Batten, Barton, Durstine and Osborne (BBDO) in San Francisco, took a shot at all those people who get hung up with the "rules" of advertising and how they often ruin a great idea. The article was appropriately called, "Nine Ways to Improve an Ad . . . to Death."

The article starts off showing the classic Volkswagen ad (Manley 1999). However, the first rule is *Show your product as large a possible.* So the small VW in the corner now takes up most of the page. The next rule, *Don't use negative headlines,* insists that we change the headline to "Think BIG!" Oh, and notice the exclamation point. People won't understand it's exciting without the exclamation point. With the next rule, *Include the product name in the headline*, the headline becomes "Think BIG, and you'll choose Volkswagen!" Now, let's work on the visual a bit. A simple picture is kind of boring, so let's apply the next rule, *Show people enjoying the product*, and surround the car with people on horseback at a country gala. Now we're cookin'. Next, we need to fix the product itself. It hasn't changed in years, and the rule says, *Add in some "news" about your product.* So, let's invent some and change the headline to "New from Volkswagen! A '63 sizzler with new sass and skedaddle!" And talk about fixing things, that logo has to go. You can't even tell what it is. Rule number six says we should *Make the logo as big as possible*, so let's just spell it out as Volkswagen. There that takes care of two birds with one logo. Now they know who's paying for the ad. Next rule. *Avoid all unpleasant connotations about your product.* Uh, oh. That German thing. Images of WWII and all that. I've got it; we'll add an American flag and the slogan, "The All American Car." No one can take offense to that. And while we're at it, let's change the name from Volkswagen to Volkswagon. Okay, what's next. *Always tell the reader where they can buy your product.* Absolutely. Let's add a subhead that reads, "See your local friendly authorized Volkswagon dealer." We don't want people to wander into unauthorized dealers. Only one more rule to go. *Always localize your ads.* We've got to make it easy for people to find out where you can buy one, so we have to list every dealer in the area along with the phone numbers. Of course, this will take a lot of room so the car now has to be smaller. That's okay, it's an ugly car anyway. There you have it an ad that really sells.

Unfortunately, the truth is that this goes on in client meetings between clients and their agencies every day. And the end result is a convoluted, confusing, and downright ugly mess that no one will read, let alone respond to.

2. Creates a Driving Curiosity

The purpose of the second shiny object facet, *curiosity*, is to hold a person's attention long enough to deliver the rest of the shiny object. The overriding question becomes, "What will make your prospects want to invest their time and efforts to take a closer look?" To answer this, let's first take a look at what curiosity is.

By definition, curiosity is an eagerness to know about something or to get information. But relying solely on a sterile definition leaves out the richness that curiosity brings to life. In fact, life as we know it is owed to curiosity. Humans are the most curious creatures on earth. We search for answers even when we don't fully understand the questions. We have an insatiable desire to know what is going on over the next hill, under the next hill, in the sky above the hill, in the plants on the hill, and in the entire world. The things that are the most difficult to discover or understand make us the most curious. Where did we come from? What are we doing here? What happens after this life?

Our quest to satisfy our curiosity has lead to miraculous discoveries, as well as disastrous accidents. We deliberately put ourselves in harm's way to find out the unknown. We take immeasurable risks just to find one piece of the puzzle.

Curiosity is truly one of the great motivators in life; in fact, a person cannot be motivated to action without curiosity. We owe all our inventions, our modern lifestyle, the clothing we wear, and the very food we eat to curiosity. Daniel Berlyne, a professor of psychology at the University of Toronto from 1962–1976, spent most of his professional life conducting research about curiosity. He ultimately believed that curiosity is a motivational prerequisite for exploratory behavior and that it should be included as one of the primary biological drives (Berlyne 1960).

The good news is that if you have chosen the shiny object methodically using the shiny objects quadrants, curiosity will be almost inherent in its nature, and your target market will be naturally curious about it. However, there are many techniques you can use to accentuate curiosity. Here are a few of them.

Ask a Question

There is nothing more intriguing than asking a probing question. A well-phrased question that goes right to the core of the shiny object is an immediate lead to the rest of the shiny object facets. It's the perfect segue. But be careful that you don't ask a question that solicits an answer you don't want. The direct result of people's curiosity is an answer. If you don't quickly supply the answer, your customer will. For example, it's probably not wise to ask, "What's the most important thing in your life?" Although an engaging question, you have no idea how your prospects will answer it in their heads. As most attorneys will tell you, never ask a question unless you know how the person will respond. A famous question that shouldn't have been asked was "Wouldn't you really rather have a Buick?" A great many people said, "No."

An alternative is to ask an interesting question to which there is no answer. A recent Budweiser ad campaign asked, "Why Ask Why?" No one even knows what that really means, but it sounds interesting enough to engage your curiosity.

Here are a few notable questions used in successful ad campaigns over the years:

- "Where's the beef?"—Wendy's Hamburgers
- "What's in your wallet?"—Capital One
- "Got Milk?"—California Milk Processor Board
- "Doesn't your dog deserve ALPO?"—Alpo Dog Food
- "Does she or doesn't she?"—Clairol Hair Color
- "Is it soup yet?"—Lipton Soup
- "Is it live, or is it Memorex?"—Memorex Video Cassettes
- "Are you in good hands?"—Allstate

Make a Promise

By making a promise that is attractive to your market, you can create curiosity about how the details work. This promise can range from an actual guarantee to an outlandish, obviously unrealistic statement. The main point is that it must make your customer pause for a moment and wonder how you might fulfill the promise. If it's a real guarantee, you need to be able to immediately back it up. If it is an over-the-top statement, you need to make it clear that it is all in jest.

It's a good idea overall to be careful about what you promise. If you come across as insincere or if your claims end up causing too many questions, your shiny object can disappear very quickly. People will become focused on how you fulfill the promise rather than on the product itself. Here are a few examples of promises that have been used successfully; notice that all of them can be taken literally:

- "A-1 makes hamburgers taste like steak burgers"—A1 Steak Sauce
- "Great cheese comes from happy cows"—California Milk Advisory
- "The Power to Be Your Best"—Apple Computer
- "The mainspring in a Bulova is made to last 256 years or 146 leather straps—whichever comes first"—Bulova Watch
- "We keep your promises"—DHL
- "Good to the last drop"—Maxwell House Coffee
- "We will sell no wine before its time"—Paul Masson Wines

Tease with a Hidden Secret

Sometimes it's very effective to tease your market by giving a brief peek of your product and holding back the details for a while. Movie launches have used this technique very effectively. They often show only a scant view of what's to come as a way to create tremendous curiosity. McDonald's ran a famous teaser campaign when they introduced their Arch Deluxe burger. The campaign featured Ronald McDonald sightings at prominent events such as the Academy Awards, the Kentucky Derby, the Masters Golf Tournament, and New York fashion shows. They never mentioned the product, but instead said, "Looks like Ronald is becoming a little more grown-up." The campaign culminated with the unveiling of the adult-style burger. By most accounts, the strategy was very effective.

The biggest mistake you can make with a teaser ad is to tease for too long. Eventually, people will get either bored or frustrated. Either way, the positive curiosity turns into negative animosity. A great example of this faux pas was the original introduction of

Infiniti cars in 1989. Often referred to as the "Rocks and Trees" ads, this controversial campaign—conceived by Hill, Holliday, Connors, Cosmopulos Inc.—spent over $75 million introducing a car . . . without ever *showing* the car. Instead, it depicted various natural scenes that left most people scratching their heads wondering, "What was that all about?" There is no doubt that the ads created a stir and attracted attention to the new brand; but after seeing the ads more than a few times, most viewers began to scream, "SHOW ME THE CAR, ALREADY!"

Make a Provocative Statement

Once you've grabbed someone's attention, a great way to create a driving curiosity is to make a statement that causes people to wonder, "What did they say?" or to think, "I can't believe they just said that." A strong statement that takes an unusual position can often pull people in off the streets to see what you're doing. But be careful— all too often, companies can appear offensive in an attempt to create something provocative. Dolce & Gabbana ran an ad in 2007 that was so distasteful that it was banned by Italian publications. The ad showed a woman pinned to the ground by the wrists by a bare-chested man, with other men in the background looking on with slight sneers on their faces. This scenario looks like a depiction of gang rape to virtually anyone who sees the ad. It goes way beyond provocative and even offensive. Some people, especially those in the fashion industry, might rationalize that the ad is just trying to be edgy and is too much of a cartoon to be taken seriously. However, the ad does not look like a cartoon and has been taken *very* seriously by many organizations in multiple countries—even to the point of provoking protests in Spain and Italy. Dolce & Gabbana ultimately pulled the ad. The real question that this incites is: why subject your company and brand to so much negative criticism? Even though it might create a firestorm of publicity for a short period of time, it certainly won't be productive for the brand in the long run.

That's not to say, however, that provocative statements don't have their place. These statements, when used properly, have been successfully coined by many companies to create curiosity and drive customers to their brand. Here's a short sampling:

- "Isn't that a lot for a bottle of Scotch?" "Yes"—Chivas Regal Scotch
- "If your friendly neighborhood grocer doesn't have a jar—knock something off a shelf on the way out"—Dilly Beans
- "*Dick and Jane* is dead"—Encyclopaedia Britannica
- "Extinct is forever"—Friends of Animals
- "If you want to impress someone, put him on your Black list"—Johnny Walker Black Whiskey
- "To bring the wolves out"—Max Factor Cosmetics
- "The greatest tragedy is indifference"—The Red Cross
- "In a world full of Windows, we're handing out rocks"—BeOS Radio

Dare or Challenge

Remember when you were a kid and your friends dared you to do something—to go into a scary place, or try some crazy stunt? Well, the technique still works. A thoughtfully structured dare, based on a person's shiny object, can be almost impossible to resist—such as the following tag lines:

- "Betcha can't eat just one"—Lay's Potato chips
- "Get N or get out"—Nintendo
- "Inspire me. Surprise me. AMD me."—AMD
- "Once you go Mac. You'll never go back"—Apple Computer

- "Think outside the bun"—Taco Bell Restaurants
- "Be Fearless"—Symantec
- "Express Yourself"—AirTel Cellular Service

Personal Enjoyment

Two excellent ways to generate curiosity—your product or brand has an element of personal enjoyment or evokes images of entertainment. According to the Bureau of Labor Statistics (BLS) of the U.S. Department of Labor, in 2006, the average person spent 5.1 hours a day in leisure activities (BLS 2007). Only sleeping rated higher than this. Clearly, the quest for personal enjoyment is a top priority for most people.

Statements related to personal enjoyment can range from pampering to challenging, from soothing to stimulating, or from laid-back to extreme. It depends entirely on your product and your customer's shiny object. What works in one set of circumstances could be disastrous in another. Some people's idea of good time is snuggling up with a good book by an open fire, while others want to defy death by rock climbing up a cliff. Here's an assortment of well-known companies that are experts at satisfying peoples' desire for personal enjoyment:

- "We'll take more care of you"—British Airways
- "Vacation is a world where there are no locks on the doors or the mind or the body"—Club Med Resorts
- "Getting there is half the fun"—Cunard Steamship
- "You deserve a break today"—McDonald's
- "If it feels good then just do it"—Nike
- "Obey Your Thirst"—Sprite
- "The happiest place on earth"—Disneyland
- "We love having you here"—Hampton Inn

Say Something Funny

It is said that laughter is the best medicine. I also believe it is one of the most useful tools in creating curiosity. When you laugh, you become disarmed. When you are disarmed, you are often open to a new idea or thought. Humor is one of the most widespread techniques used in advertising around the world. People simply tend to develop positive feelings about a company that makes them smile.

That's not to say you have to create a knee-slapper to produce curiosity about your product. Sometimes all it takes is a grin to get you in. Remember, the whole objective of the shiny object facet of curiosity is to get your prospective customers to pause long enough and draw their interest in close enough so that you can give them the rest of your message.

Here's a collection of some famous—and not so famous—companies that have effectively used humor to create curiosity:

- "Only 1 out of 25 men is color blind. The other 24 just dress that way"—Mohara Suits
- "Skim milk does not come from skinny cows"—Alba Dry Milk
- "I can't believe I ate the whole thing!"—Alka-Seltzer
- "The beer that made Milwaukee jealous"—Mexican Brewery
- "So where the bloody hell are you?"—Australian Tourist Commission
- "If gas pains persist, try Volkswagen"—Volkswagen
- "It takes a licking and keeps on ticking"—Timex Corporation
- "Lipsmackin' thirstquenchin' acetastin' motivatin' good-buzzin' cooltalkin' highwalkin' fastlivin' evergivin' coolfizzin' Pepsi"—Pepsi
- "If it doesn't get all over the place, it doesn't belong in your face"—Carl's Jr.

Display Forbidden Fruits

Sex, greed, gluttony . . . you name the indulgence, and most people want it—to one degree or another. Sometimes it's just the anticipation or the fantasy of a particular extravagance that turns us on. And it doesn't have to be explicit. In fact, if you hold back and give just a peek at the indulgence, it creates a driving curiosity.

Some of the most intriguing campaigns that involve forbidden fruits are very innocent on one level and devilishly indulgent one another. Fragrance commercials, for example, can be very simple and modest in their approach, yet invoke a deep sensuality that heightens a person's curiosity. A Bulgari Pour Femme commercial features a woman dressed in an evening gown that goes from shoulder right down to the wrists. As the music plays, she dances seductively behind a sheer curtain, waving her arms and hands through the folds. The result is very tantalizing and creates a strong desire to see more. Of course, you only get glimpses—the nape of her neck, a low backline, a close-up of lips—all carefully orchestrated to peak your curiosity.

But be careful not to overindulge indulgence. Too much of a good thing comes off looking gratuitous and even offensive. This is certainly a situation where less can definitely be more. Here's a smattering of lines that several companies use to display hidden fruits:

- "Splash it all over"—Brut After Shave
- "So creamy it's almost fattening"—Burma Shave
- "Nothing comes between me and my Calvins"—Calvin Klein Jeans
- "The first time is never the best"—Campari
- "C'mon Colman's, light my fire"—Colman's Mustard
- "I dreamed I stopped traffic in my Maidenform bra"—Maidenform
- "I'm Margie. Fly me!"—National Airlines

Tap into Fear Factors

We all have fears: the fear of missing out, fear of getting in too deep, fear of running out of money, fear of losing our jobs, fear of stress at our jobs, fear of getting sick, fear of death, fear of getting lost, fear of losing, and even the fear of being afraid. Fear is a very strong driver. Tapping into a person's fear as it relates to his or her shiny object can solicit a great deal of curiosity—especially when you insinuate that you can help those fears go away.

I'm not talking about using scare tactics. Scaring someone into buying your product certainly might work for a while, but eventually, people wise up—and your brand could be irrevocably damaged. It is always better to be honest. Soap can't really make someone love you, but it can make you smell good. And if you have a fear of having body odor, certain soaps can definitely make you feel more confident. A new suit can't really get you that new job you want. But if you have a fear of making a bad first impression, a new suit can go a long way toward presenting you in a positive light.

Assuaging fears is not the exclusive property of consumer products and brands. Companies that handle business-to-business products deal with fears all day. Will the product be delivered on time? Will it meet specifications? What if I can't get the financing? Is there any liability? What happens if the proposal is late? What if we lose market share? What if the product launch is delayed? All of these are real fears, and all have real solutions. You will never find more motivated buyers than businesspeople whose fears have backed them up against a wall, desperate for a solution. They are far more than curious. They demand to know more!

Here are some companies that tap into fears and create curiosity by providing a possible solution:

- "Even your best friends won't tell you"—Listerine Mouthwash
- "Don't leave home without it"—American Express

- "Live today. Tomorrow will cost more"—Pan Am World Airways
- "For years we've been making our products as if lives depend on them"—Squib
- "You can trust your car to the man who wears the star"—Texaco
- "Have you ever wished you were better informed?"—The *Times*
- "You're not fully clean until you're Zestfully clean"—Zest Soap

3. Stimulates an Irrepressible Urge to Touch

The third shiny object facet is about getting the customer to take action to draw them deeper into the shiny object. The driving question related to this facet is "How do you get your prospects to reach out and try your product?"

Physical shiny objects have a psychological effect of enticing physical contact. There are basically two reasons for this. First, touch is our strongest sense to establish reality. We can smell something, hear something, even see it, and it still may not be real. But if we can touch it, we are more apt to accept its existence. For this reason, we are drawn to reach out and touch shiny objects to connect with them and determine their reality.

The second motivation for touching shiny objects is the anticipation of a positive experience with that object. As was mentioned earlier, some researchers believe we associate shiny objects with water and subconsciously are drawn to them for survival. These studies show, in fact, that infants commonly lick and mouth shiny objects much more often than dull objects. In touching a shiny object, we often discover it to be smooth and cool. This pleasant encounter is imprinted on our brain neurons and is replayed each time we see a new shiny object. When we touch another shiny object, the expectation is fulfilled and the attraction is strengthened. This cycle repeats itself over and over until it becomes part of our psyche.

In the world of marketing, the term "touch" primarily has to do with trying out a product or service. However, physical touch can, and often is, an integral part of this process. Whether it's feeling the leather trim on a car's steering wheel or clicking a mouse while trying out some new software, physical interaction with the product is often a key element of completing a sale. In fact, for many products, such as cars, software, food, clothing, shoes, TVs, houses, furniture, and musical instruments, the prospective customer demands to touch the product before committing to a purchase.

So, the key question remains: "How do you get your prospects to reach out and try your product?" Although there are new and inventive ways created every day to get someone to touch your product, there are several methods that are tried and true that have been used since people started selling stuff. Sometimes people insist on a brand-new idea, as though somehow it will work better. However, unless you have covered the basics with the proven techniques, your money is not well spent branching out into unproven territories.

Make an Offer

By providing a value incentive, you can entice your prospective customer to touch your product. You'll notice that I did not say, "providing a discount." Certainly, offering a reduced price is one way to get people to take action and try your product, but it is not the only type of compelling offer. The key point is to create an offer that provides significant value, whether that value is in the form of cash, credits, or add-on services and products. Keep in mind that the objective is to get people to purchase your product for the first time. Hopefully, once they try your product, assuming it is everything you say it is, the customers will not need ongoing enticements to make repeat purchases. Here are a few time-proven offer-oriented tactics.

Coupons and Discounts   This is a great way to get price-sensitive prospects to make a purchase. If carefully distributed to target segments, you can provide an incentive to price-sensitive customers while selling the product at full price to your mainstream customers. The other benefits of using coupons are that you can control the timing, motivate customers to switch to your brand, and control the distribution. You can also use coupons to up sell your current customers to higher-end products.

   There are also several negative points regarding coupons that need to be carefully considered. First of all, you can't control the redemption timing. Of course you can set an expiration date, but that does not control when people will actually come in to redeem the coupon. Some companies have experimented with coupons that are only redeemable during certain hours or on certain days. However, this tends to confuse the customer and ends up causing more problems that it's worth. The second drawback on coupons is they often have a way of cannibalizing your existing sales. This occurs when your current customers use the coupon to buy products they would have bought anyway at full price. Because you end up losing margin with your current customers, you better create enough new customers to make it worth your while. Another significant concern with coupons is the cost to print and distribute. Whether you are doing a direct mail piece, door hanger, or newspaper insert, the cost can often be prohibitive. There are services that combine coupons together and mail them as a package that reduces the cost, but then you have to compete with all the other coupons for attention. E-mail coupons cost virtually nothing to distribute but people are reluctant to take the time and energy to print them out. Finally, fraud is a serious concern, especially with Internet coupons. This can cost retailers thousands of dollars. These days, with so many people owning scanners and drawing software, it's pretty simple to duplicate a coupon. This completely destroys your control of your potential liability.

DANGER! DANGER! The negative side of coupons listed previously pales in comparison to this final warning: *Do not overuse coupons!* If you repeatedly use coupons to drive in customers, eventually, your entire brand will be price driven. People will simply wait until the next coupon. I have seen this practice completely destroy brands. Our agency was once brought in to create advertising for a restaurant chain in Southern California. The restaurant was recently purchased by a larger company as part of a combined deal. Frankly the restaurant was a bit of stepchild. The top executives were desperate to show positive sales to the parent company. Unfortunately, their motivation was not so much to create a stronger brand but to show a better balance. To drive up sales, they embarked on a coupon campaign. Coupons are a mainstay of many casual dining restaurants, and they are certainly a viable means to boost sales and profits when used judiciously. However, sometime around the third major coupon push in less than six months, we strongly advised them they were adversely altering the brand. Prior to this, the brand had always been know for great quality food at a reasonable price. Despite our warnings they continued to offer deep discounts. In less than two years, their market became completely dependent on coupons. Every time they stopped running coupons, their sales plummeted and stayed at the abyss. The moment they sent out more coupons, sales shot up again. Once on this coupon drug, it is extremely hard to get off. Profits drop, and the inclination is to create more sales. But with the reduced margin, the profits continue to drop. It is a destructive, downward spiral, and to pull out of it is expensive and difficult. So BE WARNED. Do not overuse coupons unless you intentionally want your brand to be discount oriented.

Rebates   These work the same way as up-front discounts except the customer must purchase the product first. Some rebates require the purchaser to mail in the forms while others are instant in the store.

Too often, the mail-in variety are very confusing, require proofs of purchase and bar codes, along with receipts. For many people, they are just too much of a hassle to deal with. However, for retailers and their suppliers, this turns out to be one of the pros of rebates. Since all rebates expire, and there are a great many people who don't file for the rebates, a manufacturer or retailer can receive the benefits of offering a discount without having to actually give one. An article in *BusinessWeek* (Grow 2005) cited a Mr. Peter S. Kastner, director of consulting firm Vericours, who reported that 40 percent of all rebates go unclaimed. This equates to roughly $2 billion in additional revenue to retailers and manufacturers.

Combos Rather than directly discounting the product, sometimes a better alternative is to offer a combination deal, such as a Buy One Get One Free, or offering a complementary product, such as free popcorn with the purchase of a movie ticket. This is a great way to offer value without having to actually reduce the price. Especially effective is the tactic to offer an add-on product along with the purchase, such as free mp3 downloads with the purchase of an mp3 player. This, in fact, actually increases the value of the product. Manufacturers and retailers can offer add-ons all day long without degrading the value of the brand. Cellular carrier companies have made a science out of this tactic. They spend millions of dollars in advertising to convince people that their network is the best, and the last thing in the world they want is to devalue it. So, instead of offering discounts on their service, they either create package deals of different services or they heavily discount the phones. In many cases, if you sign up for an extended contract, you can actually get the phone for free. A free phone if you choose their service? This approach significantly increases their value. This idea of add-on value is very effective in business-to-business marketing. A company that tries to compete by simply offering a lower price runs the risk of a competitor undercutting them. Someone can always offer a lower price, and if your brand is based on price sensitivity, it is in a precarious position. Alternatively, if your products are never discounted but bundled with other produces and services, you increase the perceived value of your brand while still offering overall savings.

Hand Out Samples

Sampling has always been an excellent method to motivate product trial. This is especially true for in-store sampling. A research analysis conducted by BIGresearch in September of 2006, indicated that "Product sampling is the most influential in-store marketing method when it comes to influencing consumer purchase decisions, and is a reliable option for marketers looking to increase ROI." According to the study (*Simultaneous Media Usage Survey*), 52.4 percent of adults 18 and older said they were either "influenced" or "greatly influenced" by in-store product sampling.

Other forms of sampling include door-to-door, direct mail, newspaper, and on package. On-package sampling is particularly effective because the customer has just committed to purchase one product and becomes exposed to another that either augments his or her experience or is related to it. Event-based sampling is also very effective. Restaurants often participate in local fairs or Taste Offs (such as Taste of Atlanta, Taste of Dallas, Taste of Los Angeles) to promote their menu by preparing and handing out free samples. Other event-based sampling occurs when large venues pull together large numbers of people, making it very economical to distribute large numbers of samples.

Provide a Demonstration

> *What we hear, we forget. What we see, we remember. And what we do, we understand.*
>
> **—Ancient Chinese Proverb**

Typically reserved for more expensive items or products that require a personal evaluation before purchasing, demonstrations can be extremely useful in motivating your customers to reach out and touch your product. There is nothing quite as convincing as having someone actually get "behind the wheel" of your product. This tactic can be particularly useful at trade shows and other events where there are large concentrations of prospective customers. Wherever you present a demonstration, the key is to give it proper prominence. Rather than putting it over in the corner in the hopes that someone will see it and ask about it, put it center stage. Make it the hero. Be bold in your efforts to draw attention to it. By doing so, the demonstration itself becomes the element that entices your potential market to reach out and touch your product.

One word of advice: make the demonstration time appropriate for the setting. In some cases, a demonstration can be over an hour long and used to close the sale. In other cases, you will be lucky to have a person commit 30 seconds of his or her time. Carefully evaluate the environment in which the demonstration will be held and the objectives of the presentation—what is required to achieve those objectives? In some instances, you might actually have to schedule a demonstration, if it is complicated and involved in nature. Also, there are circumstances when you may need to take the demonstration on the road to get people to touch your product. Mobile demonstration units are often an effective way to take the demonstration to the customer. Over the years, companies that manufacture large or expensive products have used these mobile units to effectively engage their customers.

Hold a Seminar

People love free information, especially when it has a high-perceived value. Free seminars have been a standard practice for many years to bring people together to touch your product. Surprisingly, the cost and risks are very low. The primary investment is in advertising the event and paying the deposit on the room. If not enough people sign up for the seminar to be worthwhile, you simply cancel or reschedule it and inform the registrants of the change. On the flip side, the potential benefits are enormous. Imagine a setting where you have your prospective customers captured for several hours.

The key to a successful seminar is to provide valuable information but not so much that the attendees won't need your product or service. The other element is to maintain an air of objectivity. The last thing you want is a seminar that is perceived as a two-hour commercial. You might get away with it a few times, but once you get a bad reputation, it is almost impossible to restart. One successful technique to maintain objectivity is to bring in outside speakers. We once put together a seminar for a client, Nantucket Software, which lasted *two days*. During that time, our client did not make a single presentation or pitch. Instead, they called on their contacts in the industry and assembled an impressive roster of experts. We made it very clear that the seminar was hosted and conducted by our client and, of course, all the topics were hand picked to lead the attendees to deduce that our client's product was the solution to many of the problems presented. The end result was that the attendees changed their perception about our client and a significant volume of qualified leads was produced. Based on this success, the seminar became a regular annual event for several years.

Let Them Have It for Free for a While

The next best thing to owning something you're interested in, is owning it for a little while. Hundreds of companies have been very successful at convincing their prospective customers to touch their products by offering free trials that automatically expire after a determined length of time. Software companies routinely use this method to entice sales. In some instances, the product automatically rolls over into a purchase, while others simply shut down. Still others allow you to use only a part of the product; they lead you right up to the water and, just when you're dying to drink, they cut off the stream. "To activate this feature, simply click here." A quick click, a verification of a credit card, and off you go. Instant gratification.

There are very few negatives to free trials. Perhaps the largest downside occurs if you are offering a service that has labor attached to it. The obvious risk is your time investment. For most other products and services, the downside is convincing people to participate. For example, if your product is a tangible product, you need to obtain the customer's credit card number in case they don't return the product. Some people are reluctant to enter into such an arrangement. Another potential negative is the reluctance of a prospect to go along with the free offer for fear that the company will be hounding them for a purchase or that the company will somehow charge them at the end of the free trial period. However, these downsides are minimal compared to the benefits received from offering free trials. If your product lends itself for a free trial, it is always worth considering.

4. Activates an Emotion

The fourth shiny object facet is all about getting people to experience your brand, product, or service, not just to try it. The driving question is "Which emotions evoked by interaction with my product will lead to a sale?"

Every purchase, no matter how technical or rational, has an emotional factor. Over the years, I have successfully marketed semiconductors, medical equipment, electronic test equipment, financial institutions, property management companies, title insurance, malpractice insurance, and host of other products that might seem to have no bearing on emotions. However, these companies were all successful in their marketing because they discovered the right emotion button that related to their product.

An article published by Knowledge@Emory (2008) cites Liam Fahey, chief architect at Emotion Mining Company, whose background includes neuroscience, medicine, and psychiatry. Mr. Fahey stated, "When it comes to deconstructing the customer experience, all too often emotions are not carefully considered. This is especially surprising because every customer experience stimulates emotions. Seeing an ad on TV, using a product, or engaging with a salesperson may spawn an array of feelings." He went on to explain that so-called "rational" purchase decisions are "always influenced, and are often driven, by emotional considerations."

In Book Two of Aristotle's *Rhetoric*, written sometime around 335 BC, Aristotle endeavored to define emotions. In his analysis, he grouped emotions into seven opposing pairs and postulated that all human emotions could neatly fit into these pairs. Every emotion was accompanied by a corresponding pain or pleasure. This was the very first attempt to analyze emotions and, although many other philosophers and psychologists had expanded and revised the list, Aristotle's basic premise still remains intact. It's important to note that Aristotle's deductions were affected by the social perceptions of his time. For example, ancient Greeks thought anger was the result of being slighted by an inferior. It was therefore believed that slaves were incapable of anger since they had no inferiors (Aristotle 1984, 92–120).

Aristotle's List of Emotions

Emotion	Definition
Anger	An impulse to revenge that shall be evident and caused by an obvious, unjustified slight with respect to the individual or his friends. Slights have three species: contempt, spite, and insolence.

Emotion	Definition
Mildness	The settling down and quieting of anger.
Love	Wishing for a person those things which you consider to be good—wishing them for his sake and not your own—and tending so far as you can to affect them.
Hatred	Whereas anger is excited by offenses that concern the individual, hatred may arise without regard to the individual as such. Anger is directed against the individual, hatred is directed against the class as well.
Fear	A pain or disturbance arising from a mental image of impending evil of a painful or destructive sort.
Confidence	The hope (anticipation), accompanied by a mental image, of things conducive to safety as being near at hand, while causes of fear seem to be either nonexistent or far away.
Shame	A pain or disturbance regarding that class of evils, in the present, past, or future, which we think will tend to our discredit.
Shamelessness	A certain contempt or indifference regarding the said evils.
Benevolence	The emotion toward disinterested kindness in doing or returning good to another or to all others; the same term represents the kind action as an action; or the kind thing done considered as a result.
Pity	A sense of pain at what we take to be an evil of a destructive or painful kind, which befalls one who does not deserve it, which we think we ourselves or someone allied to us might likewise suffer, and when this possibility seems near at hand.
Indignation	A pain at the sight of undeserved good fortune.
Envy	A disturbing pain directed at the good fortune of an equal. The pain is felt not because one desires something, but because the other persons have it.

(Continued)

Emotion	Definition
Emulation	A pain at what we take to be the presence, in the case of persons who are by nature like us, of goods that are desirable and are possible for us to attain—a pain felt, not because the other persons have these goods, but because we do not have them as well.
Contempt	Persons who are in a position to emulate or to be emulated must tend to feel contempt for those who are subject to any evils (defects and disadvantages) that are opposite to the goods arousing emulation, and to feel it with respect to these evils.

Source: Hauser n.d.

Since Aristotle's time, there has been tremendous disagreement regarding the definition of the basic emotions. In 1990, A. Ortony and T. J. Turner compiled a list of the various theorists and their views about which emotions were basic:

Theorist	Basic Emotions
Arnold (1960)	Anger, aversion, courage, dejection, desire, despair, fear, hate, hope, love, sadness
Ekman, Friesen, & Ellsworth (1982)	Anger, disgust, fear, joy, sadness, surprise
Frijda (personal communication, September 8, 1986)	Desire, happiness, interest, surprise, wonder, sorrow
Gray (1982)	Rage and terror, anxiety, joy
Izard (1971)	Anger, contempt, disgust, distress, fear, guilt, interest, joy, shame, surprise
James (1884)	Fear, grief, love, rage
McDougall (1926)	Anger, disgust, elation, fear, subjection, tender-emotion, wonder
Mowrer (1960)	Pain, pleasure
Oatley & Johnson-Laird (1987)	Anger, disgust, anxiety, happiness, sadness

Theorist	Basic Emotions
Panksepp (1982)	Expectancy, fear, rage, panic
Plutchik (1980)	Acceptance, anger, anticipation, disgust, joy, fear, sadness, surprise
Tomkins (1984)	Anger, interest, contempt, disgust, distress, fear, joy, shame, surprise
Watson (1930)	Fear, love, rage
Weiner & Graham (1984)	Happiness, sadness

It is very difficult to describe an emotion with a word. There are an infinite number of nuances that makes each emotion different. As a result, the English language is replete with hundreds of words used to describe emotions. Below is a sampling:

Acceptance	Bitter	Delighted
Adoration	Bored	Delirious
Affection	Breathless	Depression
Agitated	Calm	Desire
Amazed	Cautious	Despair
Amused	Cheerful	Determined
Anger	Cold	Devastated
Annoyed	Compassionate	Disappointed
Anticipation	Concerned	Discouraged
Anxiousness	Confident	Disgust
Appreciative	Contempt	Dispirited
Ardent	Courageous	Eager
Aroused	Cowardly	Ecstatic
Ashamed	Crafty	Embarrassed
Astonished	Curious	Emphatic
Awed	Cynic	Enraged
Bewildered	Dejected	Enthusiastic

Envy	Intimidated	Playful
Euphoric	Irate	Pleased
Excited	Irritated	Pride
Exhausted	Jaded	Puzzled
Fascinated	Jealousy	Rage
Fear	Joy	Relief
Foolish	Lively	Remorse
Frazzled	Loathsome	Resentment
Frustrated	Lonely	Sadness
Furious	Longing	Scared
Giddy	Love	Sensual
Gleeful	Loyal	Sexy
Gloomy	Lust	Shame
Grateful	Mean	Shocked
Greedy	Melancholic	Sincerity
Grief	Mellow	Somber
Grouchy	Miserable	Sorrow
Happy	Morbid	Sorry
Hate	Mourning	Stressed
Heartbroken	Nervous	Strong
Homesick	Offended	Surprised
Hopeful	Optimistic	Sympathetic
Hopeless	Outraged	Terrified
Horrified	Overwhelmed	Threatened
Hostile	Pacified	Thrilled
Humiliated	Pain	Trust
Hurt	Panicky	Uncertainty
Indignation	Paranoia	Uneasiness
Infuriated	Passion	Unhappy
Inner Peace	Peaceful	Vengeful
Insecure	Perturbation	Vicious
Inspired	Pessimistic	Worried
Interest	Pity	Worthless

How Do You Choose?

Excellent question. The fact is—you shouldn't choose which emotions would engender a sale; your customers should. Shiny Object Marketing is all about your customers, not your product or company. It is up to them to determine what will motivate them to take out their wallets.

The first step is to go back to the shiny objects you identified. These provide the pathway to selling your product. By focusing on the shiny objects, it is easier to determine which emotions are related to them. For example, let's say you have determined your customers' shiny objects are *making their lives* easier and *social acceptance by their peers.* It is very likely that one or more of the following emotions can tap into these shiny objects:

Acceptance	Envy	Inspired
Adoration	Euphoric	Joy
Appreciative	Excited	Lazy
Cheerful	Gleeful	Pleased
Confident	Grateful	Pleasure
Determined	Gratified	Pride
Enthusiastic	Happy	Relief

Once you have made an initial determination of what the emotions might be, it's time to take them to your customers and prospects. I typically advise my clients to take a two-step approach to accomplish this:

Step 1—Focus Group

Focus groups are not very effective or reliable at providing answers, but they are wonderful for generating ideas and questions. All too often, clients conduct a focus group and use the information as though it is the definitive approach. Even holding 10 focus groups at different locations across the country would still only give you a very small sampling of the market. Plus, focus groups are biased by their very natures. It takes a certain mindset to take time out of the day to sit with a bunch of strangers, answering questions about a product that you really don't care much about. So, it's important to use the focus group in the most effective way. Take your preliminary list of emotions and find out the group's reaction. You will probably find that you are way off on some emotions and have completely missed others.

As far as the profile of the attendees of the focus group, I always suggest two separate groups: one group of people who have purchased your product and a second group that considered purchasing it, but for one reason or another chose not to. The customers' group can shed light on exactly which emotions bubbled up when they purchased your product. The noncustomers will be able to give you an equally illuminative perspective on the emotions that caused them *not* to buy your product. Any professional focus group facility can help you with the recruitment of these attendees. You simply need to tell them the profile of who you want to attend, and they will go find them.

Step 2—Quantified Study

Once you have narrowed down the list of emotions based on what your customers and prospects have chosen, you need to take it to a broad spectrum of people to produce a quantifiable and accurate projection to your entire market. There are a variety of methods to accomplish this including Internet surveys, mall intercepts, phone interviews, and direct mail questionnaires. The research company you choose can help you select which method will best accomplish your objectives, based on your product and market segment.

Let me provide a few examples that illustrate the power that emotional appeal can have over purchases that are seemingly void of emotion. The first comes from my experience with a mortgage company. I worked in a boiler-room environment. There were about 40 salespeople hunkered down in row after row of cubicles. The team consisted of men and women from all races and ranged in age from 25 to 65. It represented a fairly good cross-section of the population. Their job was to answer the phones and try to get the callers to submit an application for a home loan. They all had the same tools and training. However, some people achieved tremendous success, while others barely squeaked by. You would think that the people who called in were going to make their decision strictly on rationale. Mortgages are all about rates and terms; therefore, emotions would not seem to be a part of the equation. But the way it turned out was *quite* the opposite. Salespeople were not successful because of pressure tactics or their ability to impress people with their knowledge of the mortgage industry. The secret was in the personality of the salesperson. The people who rose to the top were able to quickly identify the customers' shiny objects and relate to them. The call wasn't so much about the loan as it was about the shiny object and how the loan could help the customers. There was one salesperson in particular who was making over $10,000 a month—and even over the phone, he was the nicest guy you could ever meet. He had an amazing ability to bring the conversation immediately to the shiny object and tap into the customers' emotions. Once he did that, customers almost immediately filled out the application; and he was on to the next call. He wasn't phony, glib, or particularly smooth. Quite the opposite—he came across as concerned, caring, and helpful. To top it off, he kept excellent notes so that every time a customer called back he could instantly relate back to that person's shiny object. Rates and terms became completely secondary to being treated like a real person with real emotions.

The next scenario comes from the files of my past clients. This was probably one of the most technical sales with which I have ever been involved. The product was a machine that removed pollutants—particularly methyl tertiary butyl ether (MTBE), which is a government-mandated fuel additive, and other volatile organic compounds (VOCs)—from groundwater. The company was called Advanced Phase Separation, and their market was primarily city engineers and environmental consultants. Both of these groups would go through exhaustive research and analysis before recommending such a system. It required months of evaluation, and the specifications had to be right on the nose. Sounds like a fairly unemotional appeal, correct? Well, our client certainly thought so. When they first began to market the product, they sent a mailing to over 1,000 contacts that did an outstanding job of pinpointing the features and benefits of the system. However, despite the well-executed plan, the mailers produced a whopping 0 percent return. Not a single person responded. That's about the time we became involved.

We started over and based the program on the Shiny Objects Marketing concept. We identified the shiny objects of their customers to be (a) making the right decision and (b) making life easier by using a simple process. Based on this assessment, we determined two emotional appeals: (1) the fear of making a bad decision and costing the city millions of dollars (not to mention losing their jobs) and (2) the comfort of dealing with a technology that is easy to understand and use. We built an entire campaign around these two emotions and created the tagline: "Simple Science for Cleaner Water." We even changed the name of the product from APS to Simplex to emphasize the point that this process was extremely simple. The results were predictable, but the client was astounded. The very first mailing based on this direction produced a 10 percent return. And several of those leads turned into million dollar contracts. Not bad for a product that had no emotional appeal!

A final situation that depicts how an emotional appeal is critical even in the most rational of purchasing processes comes from a client whose industry often has to deal with contentious circumstances. It is a property management company named Professional Community Management (PCM), and it works with homeowner associations. PCM's primary role is to carry out the wishes of the association's board of directors; but they are often—and incorrectly—perceived as the ones running the show. If a homeowner takes umbrage with an issue—such as the maintenance of the common grounds, or enforcing the rules and regulations—he will often blame the property management company, even though the management company is strictly working under the direction of the board. The members of the board have a direct fiduciary responsibility to the association and its homeowners and must ensure that the property management company is properly fulfilling its contract. For this reason, the board members usually take their role quite seriously. When it comes time to search for a property management company, the board is obligated to complete a thorough due diligence process. They investigate rates, services included, contracts managed, vendors coordinated, and maintenance schedules. However, when all the comparative work has been done and two or more companies qualify, it comes down to the one with which the board *feels* most comfortable. Not very rational or calculable, but the deciding factor nonetheless.

In working with PCM, we investigated the emotional appeals used by the competition. They ranged from "The company that improves the quality of your life," to "The company that has the Spirit of Community." After researching the emotions expressed by the homeowners, however, we discovered that they didn't believe a property management company could really improve their lives. Instead, they expressed *sentiments* that they *felt* more comfortable with, a company that lived up to its promises and simply completed the job that it was hired to do. Coincidentally, this is exactly what PCM excelled at: taking the job assigned to them and making sure it happened on time and on budget. Based on this, we coined the line, "We Get It Done," which PCM started using on all literature and sales presentations.

The appeal worked. It resonated with homeowners and boards alike. It helped create a unique competitive advantage and significantly benefited their sales process. According to Donald Disbro, Vice President, New Business Development and Marketing for PCM,

> Our clients want to have complete trust in our abilities and our word. When we say we will do something, it is absolutely critical that we "Get It Done" in order to earn that trust. Our slogan is more than a clever catch phrase. It embodies the philosophy and culture of our company. Because in the final analysis, after the proposal has been rigorously reviewed by the board, they have to *feel* confident, that we will do the job.

These examples show that there is an emotional appeal even in situations where the decision process is considered to be clinical, logical, and methodical. It simply can't be avoided. Human beings will always inject some sort of emotional behavior into every decision process.

For the Unbelievers　　For those who are reluctant to believe that emotions play into all purchases, consider the following: You have a product that you believe has absolutely no emotional appeal. Let's say that it's a military specification (mil spec) electronics connector that you sell to defense and aerospace contractors. As such, like all mil spec parts, there is no room for altering the specification. Cut and dried, right? The buyer's decision all comes down to price, delivery, and meeting the specification, correct? Okay, let's say you get through the proposal process: all your drawings have been approved, the connector has passed testing, and you have met the price and delivery demands. So far, so good. No emotions in play here. Now let's say that the aerospace contractor calls your chief engineer with some additional questions, and your engineer—having just heard that his son crashed his new BMW through the garage door—is uncharacteristically rude. So, rude, in fact that he basically tells the aerospace contractor where he can stuff it. Do you believe that the deal will sail right through according to schedule? Most likely not. Why? The aerospace contractor is human. He reacted to the emotional outburst of your engineer, and he responded with an outburst of his own. This interchange reflected poorly on your entire organization and could sour the entire deal. At the very least, you've got some damage control to do.

Bottom line—you are better off considering the emotion that might be related to your customer's shiny object than taking a risk and assuming that your purchase process is emotion free—because really, none ever are.

5. Demands Ownership

The purpose of the fifth and final shiny object facet is not to just sell your product, but to create such a strong relationship between your product and your customer that the customer literally *demands* ownership. Your customer absolutely has to have your product, brand, or service. The driving question here is, "What will make your prospects want to grab your product and not let go?"

Let's Be Negative

Sometimes the best way to understand how something works is to come from the negative direction: figure out what keeps it from working. This is definitely true with the fifth shiny object facet. To determine how to motivate your prospects to become ardent customers, it's important to understand what is stopping them from being customers in the first place. I often use the analogy of a door to represent the sales process while working with my clients. Right now, the prospective customer stands at a door that is not only closed, it is also locked. On the other side of the door is a blissful relationship with your product. Your challenge is to first figure out what the doors consists of, and then determine what the key to unlocking it is.

This "closed door" exercise works best in a group environment where you can glean information from a wide range of perspectives. This type of setting also allows you to delve into interesting directions as they are talked about. It is also very useful to conduct this exercise with customers, prospects, and employees. To give you an idea of how it might go, I've provided a list of doors and the corresponding keys that were identified at a Shiny Objects Workshop that I conducted.

Door	Keys
Reputation of just being a commodity product	Consistent service Consistent message Testimonials Case studies Brand repositioning Advertising Public relations
The company name connotes old technology	Connect with a strong descriptor Create a strong tagline to reposition company Enhance the name through service offering
Getting past the gatekeeper	Training Key prospect campaign Visibility in the community Bring gatekeeper in as part of the process Make sure the message is to the right audience

Door	Keys
Resistance to price	Sell value not price Return on investment analysis Get early in design stage Sell solutions not products Sell partnership
Prospects are unsure of the nature of service	Get the word out Clear, concise message Sales training
Lack of confidence in the company	Testimonials Share success stories that match the industry Demonstrate expertise Do your homework We're part of a large resource
Salespeople resistant to changing their paradigm	Education Training Show how to make money Market it within the system
Poor economy or limited budget	Show they'll get better Return on investment Efficient use of budget Measurable/immediate results
Marketplace not ready	Help them to see that they are ready Focus on industries where we have expertise

Let's Get Positive

So now that we know the issues and how to get past them, we are ready to take the next step—which entails cementing the bond between your product and your customer. To truly make your customers want to grab your product and not let go, you need to make them feel so comfortable with and reassured by your brand, product, or service that they would be afraid to go anywhere else.

One more time, let's consider the raccoon—one of the most intelligent, clever, and resourceful animals you can find. They can open locks, undo latches, open doors, and untie knots. If they can't find their way through or under a fence, they'll look for a tree branch to climb up and find access over the roof. They are by no means dumb. Yet they will reach through a hole for a shiny object, grab it, and become trapped because their paw grasping the object is too big to pull back through the hole. Why do they do this? Clearly, it's not because they are dimwits. The simple fact is that once the raccoon has achieved possession of the shiny object, he is afraid to let it go—possibly fearing that he might lose it forever.

So, how do you engender that kind of fanaticism about your product? Here are a few ideas:

- *Product, brand, or service meets or exceeds its promise:* Let's start with the basics. If you make outlandish promises that you can't keep, you will never create fans. As Abraham Lincoln said, "You can fool some of the people all of the time, and all of the people some of the time, but you can not fool all of the people all of the time." This is not to say that every product has to be of premium quality; after all, not every car is a Mercedes. However, the promise must fit the facts. If it is a cheap product that works for a while and then self-destructs, say so and price it accordingly. There is always a huge market for products like this, and people are genuinely okay if the investment matches the value. But don't give the impression that $1.50 will buy something that will become a family heirloom for generations to come. Also, even if your product is competitive but not top of the line, you can create a powerful brand by going above and beyond a person's expectations.

- *Immediacy:* You've got to get it now. It may seem crude, but creating immediacy and urgency around your product is an effective way to create a demand for it. Keep in mind, however, that we are not just creating the desire to grab your product—but to *not let go* as well. To do this, the immediacy has to be real. If you fabricate an artificial immediacy around your product, the customer may quickly grab it; but once they figure out they've been manipulated, they will loosen their grip. The next time a competitive product comes by they have no reason to keep a hold on yours. In contrast, a real sense of urgency might exist for a limited edition product that will truly go out of production. Or it could be for a specially reduced price that is only available for a short time because of a legitimately rare purchase. But the most effective priorities are the ones you can create around the shiny object itself. "Why put off acquiring your shiny object when you can have it right now?" This sense of immediacy does not rely on special pricing or other gimmicks. It motivates based on the inherent attributes of the shiny object.

- *Comfortable familiarity:* Once you have it, don't let it go. Comfortable familiarity is also known as brand inertia and is one of the best ways to make sure your customer will keep a strong hold on your brand, product, or service. The goal is to make your customers feel so comfortable with your product that the energy or risk required to change is simply not worth it. High-end car dealers are exceptionally skilled at this. Two days after you buy the car, they call to make sure everything is okay. A week later, they send a postcard thanking you for the purchase. A few weeks later, you start receiving a special magazine all about your car and the lifestyle associated with ownership of it. They offer free oil changes and car washes. They send you friendly reminders about service. And heaven forbid there should be a recall of a device on the car—they become extremely apologetic and do everything they can to make it convenient for you, including giving you a rental car. After all of this attention, it becomes difficult to go elsewhere.

Comfortable familiarity can also be achieved by encouraging repeat purchases through special coupons, invitations, or free samples to buy additional or supplementary products. The idea is to get the customer so involved in your brand that they have no reason to switch.

- *Uncommon courtesy:* People expect a certain level of service and courtesy in every transaction. Even when people make purchases on the Internet, they expect polite confirmations of their orders. But this common courtesy is only the entrance price to the game and, unfortunately, is sadly lacking for most companies. And to win, you have to practice *uncommon* courtesy. This is the kind of interaction that sets companies apart from the mediocre and creates a true bond between the customer and the company.

For example, many retailers have instituted the following policy for their employees to practice: when a person asks for the location of a product, the employee takes the customer to the product, instead of just pointing. Compare the difference: "Oh, yeah. It's over there on aisle 12 somewhere. Toward the end, I think. If it's not there it might be on aisle 10 or 8. I'm not sure." Or "That's right over here on aisle 12. Let me show you." Home Depot, whose vast warehouse can be daunting to the uninitiated, becomes much friendlier when a staff member acts as your guide to find the shiny object you're looking for. Vons grocery stores have realized that most supermarkets have the same goods with competitive prices. By instructing their employees to escort their customers to their products, they've singled their store out as a provider of uncommon courtesy.

You've probably come to expect the cashier at the check-out stand in most retailer stores to mumble something indistinguishable as you finalize your transactions. At Starbucks and Peet's Coffee and Tea (two companies hotly competing for the same market), you come into contact with something different. The counter person genuinely seems sincere as he or she cheerfully greets you, takes your order, and sends you on your way with uncommon courtesy.

And then there's the plumber. Often late, dirty and carrying the smells from the last job, even *common* courtesy is noticeably absent when the plumber shows up. One plumbing company in Southern California called Mike Diamond has made a name for itself by advertising the promise, "I guarantee my plumber will show up on time and smell good or your house call is free!" A little uncommon courtesy can make a huge difference.

The benefits of uncommon courtesy are by no means exclusive to consumer-oriented companies. Even high-tech and other business-to-business firms can greatly increase their customers' affinity toward their brand by practicing uncommon courtesy. I have often been the recipient of both uncommon courtesy and discourtesy. I am always drawn to the businesses that provide unique consideration toward their customers. Here are nine tips that you might put to use in your company to ensure that your employees are creating the right impression and a sense of uncommon courtesy:

1. First and foremost, return calls promptly and when you say you will.
2. Keep your word. When you make a promise to meet a deadline or perform a certain task, do whatever it takes to accomplish it. Keeping your word is the best way to foster uncommon courtesy.

3. Keep communicating. Not hearing from someone is worse than getting bad news. Keep your clients and customers constantly updated. Think about implementing a web page where your customers can look up the status of an order or project 24 hours a day.

4. Don't ever drop by unannounced. This is a surefire way to make your customers angry. It says that your time is more important than theirs and implies that they need to drop everything because you happened to stop by.

5. Don't ever assume that anytime is a good time for a meeting. Always ask your client: "Is this a good time?"

6. When possible, prepare an agenda for a meeting. This gives everyone a heads up for what's going to be discussed and allows them time to prepare.

7. Be on time for meetings. Again, never treat anyone as though his or her time is less important than yours. If you are stuck in traffic, make sure you call from your cell phone. If you don't have a cell phone, get one.

8. Be judicious in the e-mails you send and forward. According to a survey conducted by the American Marketing Association in 2003, the average employee spends over 25% of their work day dealing with emails). Don't add to the pile with funny stories or urban legends your friend sent you.

9. Make sure that everyone in your company is trained on phone etiquette. Every time someone speaks to a person outside your company, they are creating a perception about your brand.

■ *Stand up for your product—not just behind it:* It's one thing to say that your company stands behind everything it produces; but to go above and beyond and make people want to grab your product, you must stand up for your product. You must take a proactive approach and address problems before they ever arise. This includes instituting an unconditional warranty with no questions asked on your product whenever possible. To this day, Sears will replace Craftsman tools, no matter what happens to them—no questions asked. You can run them over with a tank, and they will still replace them. Obviously, if you manufacture delicate electronic machinery and your customer drops it out the back of a moving truck, you might not be able to replace it for free. But even when your customers commit such egregious acts, you must be able to help them through the crisis as best you can. It is definitely true that the customer is not always right—but you better make them feel as though they are.

It is important not to just tolerate your customers, but to become their advocate and their fan. Remember: your customers are the ones who pay for your house and the stuff inside it. They put your children through college. They pay for your vacation. They buy the car you drive. They pay for your computers, desks, and even the lease on your office. Without your customers, you wouldn't be in business. If you truly want to have customers grab a hold of your brand and not let go, this philosophy needs to permeate your company.

One company that has established itself at the apex of respect for customers is Nordstrom. At one time, they had a policy that they would accept anything back without asking any questions, no matter the condition—and whether it was even sold at the store. In 1975, Nordstrom bought a store in Anchorage, Alaska from Northern Commercial Company. A customer came into the store and, not realizing the store had changed hands, wanted to return a set of tires. Of course, Nordstrom had never sold tires; but they decided that it was not the customer's fault that the company had changed hands, so they accepted the return. For years, Nordstrom employees were welcomed into the company with an "Employee Handbook" that consisted of one 5 × 8 card that said:

> Welcome to Nordstrom. We're glad to have you with our Company. Our number one goal is to provide outstanding customer service. Set both your personal and professional goals high. We have great confidence in your ability to achieve them.
>
> **Nordstrom Rules**
> Rule #1: Use your good judgment in all situations.
> There will be no additional rules.
>
> Please feel free to ask your department manager, store manager, or division general manager any question at any time.

Over the years, Nordstrom has backed off of such an aggressive stance on customer service. But the foundation they laid for many years has built a brand that motivates customers to grab hold of their brand and not let go.

- *Sweat the small stuff:* I have nothing against Richard Carlson's book, *Don't Sweat the Small Stuff.* It is very relevant to enjoying life. However, the exact opposite is true in the world of branding. Companies win and lose lifetime customers by "sweating the small stuff." In fact, the big stuff is usually much easier to identify and take care of. The small stuff goes right down to the level of the individual employee and must be something that is ingrained into the philosophy of the company. Simple things like following up phone calls, remembering customers' name, opening the door for them, greeting them with a smile, using a pleasant voice on the phone, paying attention to detail in e-mails and proposals, and saying thanks goes a long way toward achieving the fifth shiny object facet.

We've all experienced something "small" provided by a company that has truly enhanced our dealings with them. For example, one printer that we have used for years had a salesman who would bake cookies every night and take them around to his customers as he made sales calls. It was a very simple thing—barely noticeable in the course of the day's chaos. But instead of buying donuts, he actually spent the time to bake cookies. It showed a personal commitment on his part to his customers. He was doing something nice because he appreciated their business. Obviously, major printing contracts weren't awarded because of a plate of cookies. But when the bids from several printers came in, there was definitely an affinity for the cookie man.

Polish the Five Facets

There is a saying that "Information is power." However, I believe information is worthless unless you act on that information. A shiny object doesn't usually shine just by sitting there. In fact, the opposite is quite true. Unless you pay consistent attention to the shiny object it can become dull over time to the point that your customers may not even see it. In this chapter, I presented a treasure trove of information on the five shiny object facets. If you conscientiously apply that information to your shiny object it will be truly shiny. As a recap, these five facets and their driving questions are as follows:

The Five Shiny Objects Facets

1. *Grabs your attention:* What will cause your customers to stop dead in their tracks and take notice of what you are selling?

2. *Creates a driving curiosity:* What will make your prospects want to invest their time and efforts to take a closer look?
3. *Stimulates the desire to touch:* How do you get your prospects to reach out and try your product?
4. *Activates an emotion:* Which emotions evoked by interaction with my product will lead to a sale?
5. *Demands ownership:* What will make your prospects want to grab your product and not let go?

8

Brands as Shiny Objects

All the concepts we've discussed so far throughout the book relate interchangeably to brands, products, and services. In this chapter, I concentrate specifically on how the *brand itself* can be your customer's shiny object.

Wherever you go, you are saturated with brands: through TV commercials, theater commercials, billboards, bus boards, newspaper ads, radio ads, magazine ads, direct mail, and the Internet. We even wear brands; some people have them tattooed on their bodies. Some of these brands stick, and we recognize them; but most don't. Of the thousands of brands we come in contact with every day, we only internalize a few. The rest don't represent a shiny object to us; so we either ignore them or immediately forget them after we've noticed them.

And then there are those brands that become übershiny objects: They are far bigger than the collection of individual products and services they represent. These brands have become shiny objects in and of themselves. Every time this type of brand introduces a new product, the brand followers will immediately be interested.

The perfect example of this is Disney. Every time Disney launches something new—whether a movie, a new TV show, a web site, or a line of merchandise—its followers know exactly what to expect and are immediately interested. When the Disney Channel was first introduced to cable television, there was no need to spend millions of dollars explaining to the market what its content would be. People already knew. There was never any question; it was Disney. There was no need for parents to even check it out before sitting their kids in front of it.

But the Disney brand didn't just appear by magic one day. It has been carefully orchestrated and protected. At Disneyland, employees are called "cast members" to remind them that they are constantly appearing before the public and affecting the perception of the brand. Disney has extremely strict standards on their employees' appearance and how they talk to the guests. Employees throughout the company are actively encouraged to participate in community

159

events to foster goodwill and, in turn, to strengthen the opinion of
the company as a "good citizen."

Volvos are another good example of an übershiny object. You
may not like how Volvos look, but you probably believe they are one
of the safest cars on the road. The fact is that many other cars have a
safety rating that equals or surpasses Volvo; but the advertising gurus
at Volvo have done such an excellent job of building a strong brand
that if your shiny object is safety on the road, then a Volvo is right
for you. It doesn't matter what kind of car the company produces
either. It can be a van, sedan, or a sports car. As long as it has "Volvo"
stamped on it, consumers will believe it is safe.

A third example is McDonald's. Their übershiny object is a perfect example of how the brand does not have to represent the highest quality available to be powerful. No one expects haute cuisine
when they go to McDonald's. But if your shiny object is a fairly
cheap, good-tasting meal at a casual place that your kids love going
to—then McDonald's is your place. Plus, you have a pretty good
idea what to expect when they introduce a new item. No myster-
ies. No surprises. The McDonald's brand embodies the "comfortable familiarity" that I mentioned in Chapter 7—a quality that is
an extremely strong way to motivate your customers to grab hold
of your product and not let go. The stronger you make your brand,
the shinier it becomes. Eventually the brand can actually take on a
life of its own and is almost impossible to kill. Once brightly lit, it
is very difficult to extinguish a shiny object. Shiny objects have a
strange quality. In the beginning, they can get rusty and lose their
shine quite easily. But once they attain maximum shininess, they
can almost shine forever—in spite of what people and companies
do to them. This characteristic allows brands to become so valuable
over time that they often outlive the rest of the company. Here's an
example from the television industry.

The television was invented in the United States and, at one
time, almost all TVs were manufactured there. Today, virtually no TVs

are produced in the United States. However, the brand names associated with the early days of TV are still household words. Zenith, RCA, and Philco were all giants in the industry. Through a variety of mergers, acquisitions, failures, and bankruptcies, none of these companies now exist. However, their brand names live on. Various companies have bought and sold these names several times over the last decade. In fact, it is a difficult task to keep track of who owns what. LG Electronics owns Zenith. Philco owns Philips. RCA was bought by Audiovox who bought it from Thompson who bought it from GE. But despite the brands changing hands multiple times, they still refuse to die and are worth millions of dollars. It is a testament to how resilient a shiny object can be once it reaches the übershiny object state.

There are five keys to creating a brand that is a powerful übershiny object:

1. Understand the nature of a brand.
2. Deliver on the brand promise.
3. Make the shiny object shiny.
4. Make your brand about the experience, not the product.
5. Be consistent.

Understand the Nature of a Brand

It's more than a logo. Many people confuse a company's logo with its brand. Although a logo is an integral and very important part of the brand, it is not the actual *brand*. The logo is an emblem used to illustrate the brand and give it a visual image. The brand itself is much more. It is the complete blending of the company's culture, its customers' experiences, the nature of its employees, and the way it presents itself. Overall, the brand is how your customers perceive you—from the moment the receptionist answers the phone all the way to follow-up customer service after the sale.

In establishing an übershiny object, you have to be concerned about every instance during which the customer comes into contact with the brand. This process is called brand mapping, and is very effective for identifying brand stress points. You basically chart out every point of brand contact and determine the customer's experience at that point. Once you've done this, you need to determine what the experience should be at each point to make the customer experience as positive as possible.

Brand mapping can be done through a variety of research techniques including surveys with customers, focus groups, and even customer shadowing—a process where you actually *follow* your customer around for a period of time and keep a detailed account of their reactions to your brand. Does it sound cumbersome and impractical? Well, it certainly isn't easy; but the end result is often a revelation. Using this technique, researchers essentially follow people through an average day—from the moment they wake up to the time they go to bed—and chronicle their interactions with the product in question. The results of this research offer a real-world view. It takes subjects out of the research center and puts them back into their natural setting. To overcome the artificialness of this research (very few people go through life with a researcher shadowing them) it lasts for several days. During the first few days, the subject often acts intimidated or simply uncomfortable. However, most subjects settle into the routine fairly quickly and, after a couple of days, hardly notice the researcher.

Deliver on the Brand Promise

No one likes to be lied to. Yet this is exactly what happens when a company does not live up to its brand promise. I already talked a bit about this in Chapter 7 under the fifth shiny facet, but it bears repeating. Your brand is completely subject to how well you deliver on your promise. It is based on established performance over time.

Many companies actually track their brand performance to ensure that their promise is being fulfilled. Federal Express, for example, is renowned for its tracking systems. Fed Ex promises that they will "absolutely positively" deliver the package by the date and time promised. They set their own extremely strict internal standards and measurement systems to make sure that they keep that promise.

Clearly communicating the promise is critical to delivering the brand promise. If customers have no idea what to expect from you, they have no way to measure whether you've fulfilled your promise. And if they can't figure out why they should buy from you, they will go someplace else. As such, the brand is the company's single most valuable asset. The clearer you can communicate the advantages of this asset to your customer, the stronger the asset will grow.

Sometimes it takes a bit of analysis to figure out exactly what your company's promise should be. A few years ago, an insurance company retained our agency. As with most companies, they capitalized on opportunities as they arose. Sometimes it was general liability insurance; other times it was medical malpractice insurance. After working with them for a few weeks, we helped them determine that their strongest experience was in the medical malpractice arena, specifically working with small medical groups. Furthermore they concluded that because of the long-term relationships they had with their insurance carriers and their ability to negotiate with them, they could provide substantial savings that newcomers to the field were not capable of offering. As a result, the brand promise became, "We save you money because we have the tenacity to negotiate with our carriers." Prior to using this shiny object, their sales results were hit and miss. After using this shiny object as their brand promise, they immediately began to see consistent, positive results.

Consider the financial advantages of delivering on your brand promise. When you go into a supermarket, there are rows and rows of products. You'll find hundreds of branded items and an almost equal number of generic items. Why would someone pay two to three times as much for the branded product? Because the branded product consistently delivers on its brand promise, and the consumer knows what to expect. This is not always so with the generic product. Even when the ingredients are identical, most people will still choose the branded product. Certainly, there are those shoppers who simply want the lowest price and will always go for the generic. But consider the fact that markets are in the business of selling what sells best, and generics are always fewer in number than the branded products.

Make the Shiny Object Shiny

As I mentioned in Chapter 7 under the first shiny object facet (grabs attention), your brand needs to look attractive for people to be attracted to it; and the logo is an important part of a brand's "look." Although the logo is not the *only* element of the brand, it is certainly one of the most important. People tend to relate experiences with visual cues. For example, when you see a beautiful sunset, you might be reminded of a romantic evening you had years before; or when you see a particular car, you might be reminded of a road trip your family once took. Humans tend to be very visual animals; we connect memories, thoughts, and impressions to depicted cues. Logos are intentionally created to be the image cue to the brand.

Most visual cues are more easily processed and recalled if they are simple in nature; a phenomenon that is often referred to as "retina burn." When the light bounces off an image, passes through your pupil, and bounces off the retina, it actually burns a momentary reflection. The brighter the image, the longer the residual effect. When a simple image is burned on the retina, there is very little information that the brain needs to process. More complicated images are more difficult to process. As a result, people tend to remember simpler logos more often than complicated ones. Most modern companies have recognized this trend and have revised their logos accordingly. The Nike "swoosh" is a perfect example of how a very simple design can become a very memorable logo.

As a logo becomes associated with its brand promise, the two become indistinguishable from each other. For example, when a regular Starbucks Coffee customer sees a Starbucks' logo, he can almost smell the roasted coffee beans and taste the Café Latte. The Disneyland logo conjures up feelings of family fun. The Mercedes logo brings to mind images of rich leather and top-notch customer service. These companies work very hard creating these brand impressions around their logos; and they guard them very carefully.

Make Your Brand about the Experience, Not the Product

Focus on the experience, not the product; experiences motivate people, products don't. People remember emotions and events much more readily than things. By tying a distinct familiarity to your brand, you form a connection with the customer's shiny object and create something memorable. When asked about brands, people rarely say, "They have an excellent braking system," "The noise reduction circuitry is outstanding," or "Their steaks are served at 125 degrees." Instead, people are more likely to say things like, "I really felt safe in that car," "The sound was so crystal clear," or "The steak was sizzlin' hot."

You can't always control how people will react to your marketing and advertising, but you can manage and control, to a large degree, the interaction that they have with your product. The factors that make up an outstanding experience can be measured, tracked, and reproduced. This allows you to very precisely determine how to ensure that every customer has the same experience. People can be trained, products revised, and environments established to produce consistent results.

Home Depot is a good example of a well-orchestrated experience. I have been in Home Depots across the United States, and my experience has been the same every time. The stores are always clean, well organized, well stocked, and hold an exceptional variety of products. Their salespeople are always courteous and friendly. I recently went into a Home Depot in Florida, and it was, for the most part, indistinguishable from the several I've visited in California. To create a brand experience that is so well reproduced that it is virtually the same on both sides of the country is a significant accomplishment.

An interesting point to note is that the brand experience often does not involve the product at all. Sound strange? One of my all-time favorite commercials was created by McDonald's and is called "The Big Game." At no point in the commercial do you see a hamburger. The commercial is aimed at parents and coaches who end up taking the team somewhere to eat after the game. The shiny object behind the commercial is not the food; it's making the kids happy. The commercial starts with a coach giving the kids a pep talk. The kids are looking all around, paying no attention. One of the kids spots a grasshopper, and they all jump from the bench to look at it. The coach throws up his arms, giving up. Then it shows another coach explaining a complicated play to a small boy, and the coach asks, "Do you understand what I'm saying?" The little guy just shakes his head. The coach smiles, pats him on the head, and says, "Just give the ball to Danny and tell him to run toward his dad." Toward the end, one of the kids asks, "Is it time to go to McDonald's yet, Coach?" and the coach replies, "Not yet, Tommy. When the game is over." The commercial ends with the narrator saying, "It's not so much who wins or loses that makes the day. It's where you go after the game." The final shot is the kids piling into McDonald's. A fantastic commercial that genuinely related to the shiny object of the adults.

Another great commercial that focused on the brand experience is a spot produced by Hallmark called, "Report Card." The commercial starts with a little boy coming home from school and throwing his backpack to the side of his room. His mom looks through the backpack and finds a card. When his mom asks what it is, the boy replies, "Something from Mrs. Bennet." Curious, the mom asks, "What'd she give you a card for." Paying little attention to the conversation, the boy simply says, "Because I was nice to somebody." "Who?" the mom probes. As he plays with his toys and feeds his fish, the boy continues, "Scott, a boy who comes to school just once in a while because he's sick. Can we get an armadillo?" His mom wanting to know more asks, "How were you nice to him?" The boy explains as he zooms his plane around the room, "Scott can't go out to recess and stuff so I stay in to play with him. I like him. It's no big deal." "I think it might be a big deal," the mom suggests. "Can I see your card?" She opens the card, which is from Hallmark, and reads it aloud, "You didn't have to do what you did. That's what made it so special." She turns to her son and says, "Max, do you know what this means?" "Kind of," he answers. She hugs him and says, "It means you should be very proud of yourself. I know I am." It ends with the famous slogan, "When you care enough to send the very best." Sure, it's a bit schmaltzy. It's way over the top with the emotional appeal to a mother's shiny object: her children. But it works. Hallmark cards are all about linking emotional experiences with words and pictures. Their hope is that each card will stir up a positive reaction in the recipient. This spot does an excellent job of focusing on the experience a person has when he or she receives a Hallmark card, instead of on the card itself.

Peripheral Cues

Surround your brand with elements that support the experience. Remember: people are greatly influenced by visual cues. But this is only one of the peripheral cues that can enhance your brand. These cues are referred to as *peripheral* because they are on the periphery of the message you are trying to communicate. Our senses absorb these cues, and our minds link them as integral parts of the brand. These cues include music, sound, shapes, and colors.

Peripheral cues are often so effective that many brands would not exist without them. Try to imagine Avon without the doorbell sound, Lexus without the classical music, Yahoo! without the guy singing "yahoo!," Target without the color red, Playboy without the bunny, Nike without sports, or Microsoft without the shape of a window. These cues have indeed become integral parts of the brand they represent.

Some peripheral cues, though not intended to be a permanent part of the brand, attract people to the shiny object. When Cadillac overhauled its design and introduced its new styling in 2002, it used the high-energy music of Led Zepplin to help break through the perception that Cadillacs were for the over-50 demographic. In fact, the tagline for the campaign was "breakthrough." When Apple introduced the iPod it used high-energy music and also employed an exceptionally eye-popping style that featured fluorescent colored backgrounds with silhouetted people dancing in a frenzy—while wearing a white iPod and earphones. The effect was mesmerizing and garnered immediate attention by capturing the true essence of the brand and the shiny object.

Other peripheral cues are subtler and often work in the background, augmenting the perception of the brand. Shapes, sounds, and colors can work together, like a finely tuned orchestra, to elicit a very specific impression. An advertisement for an energy drink that appeals to the shiny object of excitement, might use bright colors and sharp-pointed shapes or shapes that are chaotically scattered about the ad. Conversely, a resort hotel that is trying to relate to the shiny object of rest and relaxation, should use mild, peaceful colors and round, curved shapes or shapes that are well balanced. Check it out for yourself. The next time you get a moment, do an Internet search for "energy drink" and then one for "luxury resort." You'll notice a marked difference in the use of colors and shapes in the advertising.

Sounds are also an effective peripheral cue to augment the shiny object. A soda commercial, for example, amplifies the shiny object of thirst by spotlighting the sound of the can bursting open, the liquid gurgling as it pours over the clinking ice cubes and finishing with a flourish of fizzing. Such a commercial is completely dead without the sound effects.

Be Consistent

Regardless of your budget, consistency is your best tool to create an übershiny object. In fact, it is particularly critical to be consistent when you have a small budget. Smaller companies don't have the luxury to waste millions on a campaign that goes off on a tangent. They need to make sure every dollar they spend builds on the dollar before it. All elements of the campaign—advertising, direct mail, Internet, brochures, and so on—need to work in harmony.

Obviously, a well-crafted shiny object is your best tool to attract customers, but even an average shiny object can achieve significant success if the program is consistent. If you constantly change messages however, your customer will get confused and have no idea what your brand promise is.

The objective of consistency is to move the prospect along the sales process (depicted in Figure 8.1) as efficiently as possible. Every time you communicate a message to the prospect, assuming the message is on target, you advance their stage in the process. If you don't utilize a consistent message, it's almost like starting over. For example, the first step in every sale is to create awareness. People must be aware of something before they will purchase it. Perhaps the first time you communicate to them, the message only registers slightly.

Figure 8.1   Sales Process

It goes into short-term memory and may not find a foothold. If you use the same message again, presented in a slightly different package, it will still look fresh but seem familiar. Part of the previous message transferred over to the next. Each time the message is repeated, the awareness builds until the prospect develops some level of interest. If the message is always changing, there is no transference, and the prospect has to start all over again. Short-term memory is the bane of marketing.

Consistency of the message is important all the way through the process, not just at the awareness stage. The message can become more involved as the prospect comes closer to the sale but it must never stray from the shiny object foundation.

It is important to note that a "message" can come from a variety of sources. I am not talking only about advertising but the entire spectrum of communications. This includes advertising, salespeople, news media, brochures, web sites, even the receptionist—anyone and anything that can convey a message to your prospect. As I mentioned earlier, comfortable familiarity is a very effective technique to motivate your customers to hold on to your brand. To build comfortable familiarity, your message must be consistent and never changing. This allows customers to get to know you over time and feel comfortable that you won't be changing on them.

Besides a consistent message, it's equally important to be consistent in your visibility. Whatever your budget, be consistent. Be in front of your customer every day, if you can, even if it is in a small way. A letter, e-mail, or small mailer is a great way to keep yourself consistently visible in between ads or other more expensive communications. Early in my career, I worked for an electronics distributor called Marshall. At one point, sales were down, so they completely cut their advertising. There were already rumors that Marshall was on hard times, and when they went dark, the industry became convinced they were going out of business. It took them over a year to pull out of that hole and convince their customers that they were doing okay. A similar issue occurred when I was working for Beckman Instruments. Beckman had always been at all the test and measurement trade shows around the country. They didn't always have a huge booth but they were always there in some form. Then the marketing director decided to channel funds elsewhere and completely cut the trade show budget. The result was that they became conspicuous by their absence. Companies that were considering them for purchases began to think twice. It was a huge stumble.

Don't give into the temptation to cut back on advertising during hard times or quit when you think no one is responding. Unless you are in the catalog business where you expect sales every time you send a new catalog, it usually takes a long time to move a person through the sales process. It constantly amazes me how companies slash their advertising budget when they have a sales slump.

This is akin to cutting back on food when you get sick. The simple truth is the time you need advertising the most is when sales are slow. In fact, when your competition is cutting back, you have a wonderfully strategic opportunity to gain market share. Case in point: In 1933, in the depths of the Great Depression, thousands of companies were struggling to survive. Most cut back to the bare minimum. Advertising and sales budgets were almost nonexistent. Especially hurt was the banking industry and industry associated with banking, such as cash register manufactures. Prior to the Great Depression, the National Cash Register Company (NCR) had become a behemoth. In 1925, NCR went public and issued $55 million in stock, which at that time was the largest public offering in United States history. But the pressures of the Great Depression took their toll. Sales and earnings plummeted, and within four years, the company had cut the number of its employees in half. By 1931, it was almost bankrupt. New York bankers Dillon, Read, and Company, who had set up the 1925 stock sales, were ready to invade the company. In the meantime, a small upstart, originally called Computing Tabulating Recording (CTR) Corporation, which manufactured an assortment of equipment including punched card data processing equipment and scales, started to put on the steam. Despite the crippled economy, they continued to advertise, introduce new products, and exercise a strong sales campaign. This aggressive stance was a key factor in this company securing a major government contract to maintain employment data for 26 million people. Some considered this contract to be the biggest accounting operation of all time, and it certainly opened the door to many more government contracts. By 1940, this rapidly growing company had surpassed NCR in sales. Today we know this upstart as IBM. Their tenacity in tough times eventually earned them the position of one of the largest and strongest companies and brands in the world (Campbell-Kelly and Aspray 2004, 37–39; "IBM Archives, 1930s" n.d.; NCR Corporation n.d.).

The Brand as the Shiny Object

When the customer views your brand as a shiny object, you have reached the apex of Shiny Object Marketing success. You've arrived at a point where the customer becomes so attracted to your brand, that your products become automatic purchases. As I discussed in this chapter, there have been hundreds of companies that have achieved this level of being übershiny objects. However, as I pointed out, it's a tough challenge—one that requires outstanding leadership and the determination to wrap the entire company, its people, products, and services, around the brand. But it can be done, and it doesn't necessarily require millions of dollars to build such a brand.

One last example to illustrate this point: there is a company in Southern California called Primary Color. They started out in 1985 as a prepress company but have expanded to a full range of graphic art services. Over the years, they have developed an extremely shiny brand to the point that advertising agencies and graphic design firms from all over the country are attracted to Primary Color because they know the job will be done right. They are by no means a huge company with unlimited resources. They simply and consistently fulfill the shiny object. On their web site, they make this statement, which is the foundation of their brand:

> Primary Color's unrelenting commitment to high-quality standards is based on a belief that effective color management resides at the core of the graphic arts process. Every aspect of our workflow focuses on consistency, repeatability, and excellence. It defines our success.

Many companies say this, but Primary Color actually lives it. From the moment you call or e-mail them to the excellent after-service follow-up, they fully embody this shiny object. Every time Primary Color introduces a new service, you immediately know it will exemplify the brand and there will be no question regarding the quality. And here's the big point: Primary Color charges a premium for this level of quality, and people are happy to pay it because the brand has premium value.

So, don't be fooled into thinking that branding equals spending a lot of money. It's not at all about the amount of money. It's about the shiny object and making sure it is consistently shiny.

9 | What Gets in the Way of Shiny Objects?

Let's assume, at this point, that you have figured out how to make your brand, product, or service a shiny object to your customer. Let's also assume that you have taken all the right steps to make it as shiny as possible. Now your challenge is to keep it shiny. This is not an easy task. There are always well-meaning people inside and outside your company who will tug on the shiny object to take it places where it begins to lose its shine.

Blocked from View

The fastest way for a shiny object to lose its shine is to block it from the view of your customers. If they can't see it, they can't recognize it as their shiny object. Unfortunately, many companies expend tremendous resources to create a shiny object and then proceed to obscure it. Here are the top five corporate sins, as they relate to hiding shiny objects:

1. *Chasing after other opportunities:* In the natural course of business, opportunities arise. You usually can't control which opportunities come your way, but you can control which ones you respond to. All too often, companies will take their eye off the shiny object in search of another opportunity. These new opportunities often become extremely tempting and end up diverting resources from promoting the true shiny object.

2. *Using confusing jargon:* Many companies seem to love speaking in their own language, even though the customer has no idea what they are talking about. A certain amount of jargon is unavoidable, and sometimes it's even necessary, especially when you are conveying a technical message. However, in some cases, jargon is just a lazy way to say something. It takes more work, and often more creativity, to spell out what you are trying to say in simple terms. Some ads become so

full of jargon that they are no longer recognizable as English. I frequently come across this type of mumbo jumbo especially among marketing companies. You would think they would know better. Here is a typical paragraph you might find on the Internet:

We are a leading, forward-thinking marketing firm with expertise, knowledge, and know-how in the fields of market segmentation and differentiation of cross-platform initiatives. Our unique and results-driven versatility has allowed us to employ integrated marketing programs to expand our clients ROI while maintaining true brand entities. Our copy is always centered on industry-specific motivation and customer-centric optimization.

Is there a translator in the house? A company like this might have a great shiny object, but you have to spend too much time wading through their words to find it.

3. *Changing the guard:* A company goes along for several years, building brand equity and market share by consistently promoting its shiny object. Then along comes a new marketing or advertising manager. Feeling that he has to prove his worth, he starts changing things. First to go . . . the ad agency. What most marketing directors don't seem to understand is that the agency is usually the biggest champion of their brand. People within the company often mistreat the brand and pull it in all sorts of directions. It is often the agency that is the sole voice of reason. There are many occasions when replacing the agency is the absolutely right action to take. If their work is not performing or if the resources of the agency are unable to take the company to where it wants to go, then a change is likely warranted. However, the typical scenario is that the new manager simply wants to exert control over the program so

he or she arbitrarily fires the agency. This can be the quickest way to extinguish the shiny object. The new agency is going to be reluctant to pick up the torch.

4. *Messing with the shiny object:* People within a company become tired and bored with a campaign much faster than their customers and prospects do. After a while, they want to start messing with the shiny object, thinking they are "freshening it up." In reality, they are altering the very thing that is bringing in sales. Campaigns may need to change often. But not if they are working. The Energizer Battery Bunny Campaign is a great example of an idea that superseded even the people who created it. Started in 1989 by BBD Needham Worldwide out of Chicago, the campaign took on a life of its own with the bunny appearing in over 115 spots. When TBWA/Chiat/ Day took over the account, they inherited the bunny. Instead of going in a new creative direction, they wisely chose to keep the bunny going and going and going ("The Energizer Bunny" n.d.).

5. *Letting competitors steal the light:* Imitation is the sincerest form of flattery. Don't believe it. Unless you react quickly, it is one of the fastest ways to lose the lure of your shiny object. Once you are successful, you will have competition. There is no way around it. You can't avoid it. How you react to the competition determines if the shiny object you are holding out to your customers will continue to attract attention. When you are in a market by yourself or if you are garnering the top attention, it is easy to become lazy about keeping the shiny object polished. Once you are challenged with another shiny object, you need to find a way to make yours the brightest one in the room. In Chapter 11, I offer details on this subject and give specific tactics you can use to stave off the competition.

Who Changed the Road?

Sometimes the shiny object doesn't change but the way to get to it does. Several years ago, I went to a park that I had frequented as a child. My brother and I had spent many fun hours of adventure climbing the unusually shaped rocks, and I had a very clear picture in my mind of that shiny object frozen in time. Unfortunately, when I arrived at the park, I discovered that the road we took with our parents had been altered and no longer went to the rocks. It took me several hours to retrace my memories to figure out exactly where the shiny object was located. Finally, after getting out on foot and hiking down several closed and worn-out roads, I found it. There it was, exactly as I remembered it. For a while, I began to think that maybe the rocks had been demolished to make room for the park expansion. But it wasn't the shiny object that had moved, just the road to get there.

The story of Polaroid is a clear example of this principle. The shiny object never changed. It was always the desire to get photos quickly. What changed was the technology to capitalize on that shiny object. The Polaroid Corporation introduced the instant film camera to the market in 1948. In time, it became one of the hottest stocks in the country. People were amazed by the technology. Up until then, you had to send your roll of film to the developer and wait for a couple of weeks to get it back. With a Polaroid camera, you had your pictures instantly. It was amazing! However, the euphoria couldn't last forever (RosenbumTV 2007).

The road to the shiny object started changing in 1980. Noritsu of Japan introduced the first one-hour developing system, which developed and printed a roll of film for half what the same number of Polaroid prints cost. Now that consumers no longer had to wait one or two weeks to get their prints, Polaroid began to lose its appeal. The next road shift occurred in the late 1980s. Digital cameras began to become inexpensive enough for consumers to purchase. Polaroid made a conscious decision not to embrace the digital technology—a decision that ultimately destroyed the company. Eventually, consumers completely abandoned the instant film concept, and Polaroid filed for bankruptcy in 2001. It later sold off most of its business to other companies and became nothing more than an administrative shell. Most of the assets were sold to a subsidiary of Bank One, which formed a new company named Polaroid Corporation. This new company stopped making the Polaroid cameras in 2007 and announced it would cease production of the film by 2009 (Frieswick 2003, O'Neill 2002, Polaroid 2008, RosenbumTV 2007). Polaroid went from being the dominant leader in instant pictures to being almost worthless in 20 years all because it couldn't adapt to the changing road to get to the shiny object.

Selling the Product, Not the Customer

It's really easy to lose sight of the objective. I have seen presidents and owners of companies, especially when they are the founders, who are so in love with their companies and products that they truly don't care what the customers think. They believe that everyone will see the product exactly how they see it. Even to the point that they throw away the shiny object.

While working for one agency, I was hired to do research for a new company that had developed a product line of disposable cleaning cloths. Some were made for windows, others for tires. Some had special emollients to protect leather and vinyl, while others contained polymers to protect paint finishes. All in all, a very respectable line of products that truly were effective in living up to their claims. The purpose of my research was to determine which market held the highest potential for these products. What I didn't realize was that the true purpose was to validate the president's viewpoint that he had formulated months before. The president was an avid pilot, owned several planes, and spent many hours at the airfield with other pilots. He had developed this line of products specifically out of a love for private aviation. As fate would have it, the research overwhelming showed that the market with the best potential was aftermarket automotive retailers. Private aviation had a dismal showing. When we first presented the results, the president reacted tersely, suggested that the research was flawed and demanded we do it again. Being naive and not reading the signals, I complied with the demand and conducted the entire project over again. What a surprise. The results were exactly the same. This time the president became so angry that he fired us and refused to pay for the research. I later heard that he ended up trying to market his products to private aviation with dismal results. The shame of it was that his products had a brilliant shiny object. The research showed there was a ready-made market eager to purchase it. It could have been a very successful product. Unfortunately, he ignored the shiny object and put it in a bag.

Presidents aren't the only ones to make such disastrous mistakes. Many times in the course of developing a campaign, the layers of marketing and advertising people become so immersed in the minutia (media strategies, cost per thousands, affinity indexes, production schedules, budgets, etc.) that they lose sight of the shiny object. It's almost as though they are milling around the customers without paying any attention to them. Customers are waving and shouting, "Hello! I'm over here!" but everyone ignores them and goes about their daily tasks. I was once sitting in a strategy meeting with representatives of a semiconductor company in which we were discussing the pros and cons of various marketing ideas. Most of the responses were reflective of the perceptions in the room. Predictably, the discussion deteriorated into a hotly contested battle about the features of the product. Eventually, an account coordinator, relatively new to the group, innocently asked, "What about the customer? What do they want?" A very uncomfortable hush fell over the room as everyone realized she was right. We were all too embarrassed to own up to it and waited for someone else to speak. Finally, the product director started laughing, admitting she was absolutely right. We took a 10-minute break, and when we came back, we started over again—this time focused on the customer.

Keep the Pathway Clear

As this chapter has illustrated, there are many ways to block the view of the shiny object. The list can be endless, and it would be impossible to mention them all. The key point is that after spending time, effort, and money to make your brand, product, or service into a shiny object, it would be a terrible waste to let something get it its way. Your challenge is to be a guard on the watchtower and spot the problems before they block the shiny object.

10

In a Room Full of Shiny Objects, How Do You Get Yours Noticed?

Congratulations! You have identified your customer's shiny object, you've successfully achieved all five shiny object facets, and your brand has attained shiny object status. Now you enter the room to sell your products only to discover there are other shiny objects in the room. Many of them are as bright as yours. What do you do? Your customer has the potential to be attracted to the shiny object being presented by a competitor.

This is actually a good problem to have. It means you are in the game. If your product wasn't a shiny object at all, you would have something to worry about. However, at this point, you simply need to convince your customers to pay attention to you and not the competition.

To accomplish this, I have assembled nine tactics that I have successfully used over the years. Not every tactic works for every product. You need to carefully consider both the short-term strategy and long-term objectives in choosing which tactic to use:

1. *Put a bow on it.* Package it differently from your competition. Look for new and unique ways to wrap it up. It may be true that you can't tell a book by its cover. But the publication industry figured out years ago that the cover sells the book. For inspiration, take a look at Apple. Their packaging gurus are always coming up with clever and unique ways to package their products. They always stand out from their competitors before you ever open the box.

2. *Put a spotlight on it.* Create some sort of event around your product to get into public view. This is true for consumer and nonconsumer products alike. We once created a design contest for an electronics company that was really no different than the hundreds of design contests before it. The big difference was that we put together a huge event where we gave away the prize. We had the presidents of several companies attend that, in turn, drew the press. After conducting this contest for

a few years, the event became a bigger motivator for entrants than the actual prize.

3. *Put it on a velvet pillow.* Make it seem very special. While other companies simply hand their shiny object around for people to look at, you might consider requiring an appointment. You also might want to tie the product to its royal heritage to heighten its appeal. Every product has a heritage. Find out the shiny objects of its predecessors and use them to your advantage. Another way to make is special is to attach it to the superior services the customer will receive once they've purchased the product.

4. *Deny the customers access.* This might sound a little strange, but people want what they can't have. As one tactic, you might want to make your product a bit more expensive to elevate it from the rabble. You can also put people on a waiting list. Even if there is no backlog or scarcity of the product, a waiting list is like saying, "Sign up right now, and you might be lucky enough to purchase one."

5. *Shatter all the other shiny objects.* Compare and contrast your product with the competitions'. There is nothing wrong with revealing the problems in other products if there truly are problems. At the very least, you can choose those features and benefits where your product excels. There was a time when head-to-head advertising was taboo. However that all changed in the 1970s. One ad that broke the tradition was from Fiat. In fact, there were two ads. Fiat compared itself with a Porsche. The first ad simply stated, "The Fiat 124 Spider versus the Porsche 914." It showed the two cars side by side, and the copy read, "If you're in the market for a sports car under $4,000, you've probably considered the Porsche 914. And we admit it's worth considering. But before you lay out that kind of money, you should consider the Fiat 124 Spider, too." Then Fiat proceeded to lay out a case, shiny object by shiny object,

about why the Fiat is a better choice. The second ad's head-line said, "Their engines might be in the same place, but their prices aren't."

So if your competition has a weakness, go ahead and point it out. Just be prepared for them to do the same.

6. *Put it in a glass case.* Make it seem rare and unique. You can even offer a certificate of authenticity to validate its rarity. For nonconsumer products, certification is an excellent method to make sure your shiny object stands out from the crowd.

7. *Make a threat.* I don't mean threaten the customer, but create an implied ill effect if the customer doesn't buy this product. For example, "If you don't use our product, the environment will suffer." "A dollar from every purchase goes to help the starving. We can't do it without your support." "The last thing you want is to be stranded on the road somewhere because your car broke down due to an inferior product."

8. *Offer a free polish.* Once they have the shiny object, offer to shine it up for them once in a while in the form of free services such as a periodic product check-up, free inspection, upgrades, or cleanings. The main point is to stress that once your customers purchase the product, they won't be abandoned. You'll be there to make sure they continue to have a positive experience.

9. *Attach a borrowed interest.* Sometimes, there isn't anything inherent about your product that makes the shiny object any shinier than your competitions'. In these cases, you may need to borrow the interest of another shiny object and attach it to yours. For example, get a celebrity endorsement or the testimonial of an industry-known personality. You can also borrow the interest of another product that has a similar feature to yours such as, "Our car has the exact same steering

mechanism as a Ferrari." You can even use objects or situations that have a shiny object factor to attract your customers. For example, Geico Insurance is not really that much different from any other insurance company. Their shiny object is not inherently that much brighter. So, they borrowed the interest of a cool, smooth-talking, Australian-accented gecko lizard to be their spokesperson. It's strange, but it works.

It often isn't enough to simply be shiny. As discussed earlier, your product has to outshine the other shiny objects in the room. No matter which technique you use to make your shiny object stand out from the rest, it is important to make sure it is consistent with your brand. Standing out just to stand out can actually be destructive to your brand if you portray something that is contrary to your brand promise. However, carefully crafted and skillfully implemented, a strong differentiation can put you in the coveted category of successful shiny objects.

11 | Now What?

In the beginning of this book, I told you that the Shiny Objects Marketing principle is deceptively simple:

> People, as all creatures, are innately attracted to shiny objects. If you can make your brand, product, or service a shiny object to your customers and prospects, you'll be immensely successful.

By this point, I have demonstrated the nuances that make this principle a powerful concept. I have also shared with you the tools that we use in our Shiny Object Workshops, including the shiny object quadrants and the five shiny object facets to make the application of this principle practical in your business. Properly applied, these tools can change the way you market your brand, product, or service forever. In fact, they can change the way you view peoples' interaction with objects and other people. In its fullest sense, the philosophy behind Shiny Objects Marketing is applicable, not only in business, but also in people's personal lives as well.

So, now what? Now you put down this book and get to work. The best place to start is by constructing your own shiny objects quadrants. As I mentioned earlier, this is best done in a group setting, but if you have to, you can go through it by yourself. This exercise is a great way to get your mind focused. It will help you sift through the hundreds of possible shiny objects to find that one diamond that will outshine the rest. When you go through this discovery process and decide you would like to receive additional tips and advice on how to determine your customers' shiny objects and how to use them, go to our web site (www.shinyobjectsmarketing.com) and sign up for the free shiny objects newsletter.

Shiny objects are unavoidable. They are all around us and attract our attention wherever we go. Sometimes those shiny objects are real objects, such as cars, houses, or even people. Other times they are concepts like retiring or friendship. Sometimes we can ignore them. Usually, we can't. Your prospects all have shiny objects in their lives. Some of these shiny objects might be linked to the very products and services you sell. The ultimate marketing quest is to discover what those shiny objects are. Once you have identified them and figured out how your product can deliver them, you have a tremendous power.

I believe it is the responsibility of people in sales and marketing to use this power wisely and ethically. Throughout history, many people have discovered the power of the shiny object and have used it for selfish and evil purposes. Dictators often use the shiny objects of their people only to gain power over them. Some unscrupulous people at the top of large corporations manipulate shiny objects to make millions of dollars while giving nothing back to the people who they attracted to the shiny object. Still others use shiny objects to bring in customers with the sole purpose of making a quick buck and then fleeing into the shadows only to pop up somewhere else with another scheme. Throughout this book, I have stressed that this type of marketing behavior is destructive both to the consumer and the company that practices it.

Shiny Objects Marketing never implies that people are a bunch of mindless sheep. Far from it. While it is true that people often cannot control which shiny objects they are attracted to, in the end, they have the power over which shiny objects they will follow. Companies that attain the five shiny object facets and truly fulfill their brand promise have the opportunity to become great companies—or even timeless institutions. But this can only be achieved if they can relate to the shiny object that their customers choose to follow.

At this point, I am tempted to exclaim, "Good luck and may the shiniest object win!" However, the truth is, there is room for many shiny objects in the same marketplace. So, instead, I exclaim, "Get out there and let your shiny object shine!"

References

Chapter 2

Beck, B.J. Mansvelt, The Treatises of Later Han: Their Author, Sources, Contents and Place in Chinese Historiography (Sinica Leidensia, Vol 21). Brill Academic Publishers.

King, Heidi. (2000). *Rain of the moon: Silver in ancient Peru*. New York: Metropolitan Museum of Art.

Liu, Li. 2004. *The Chinese neolithic: Trajectories to early states*. Cambridge, United Kingdom: Cambridge University Press. 3–15.

Melikian, Souren. 2001. Raining silver: Symbols of ancient Peru. *International Herald Tribune*. www.iht.com/articles/2001/03/03/york.t.php (accessed February 12, 2008).

Rawls, Wilson. 1961. *Where the red fern grows*. Garden City, NY: Doubleday.

Chapter 3

Coss, Richard G., and M. Moore. 1990. All that glistens: Pt. I. Water connotations in surface finishes. *Ecological Psychology* 2: 367–380.

Coss, Richard G., S. Ruff, and T. Simms. 2003. All that glistens: Pt. II. The effects of reflective finishes on the mouthing activity of infants and toddlers. *Ecological Psychology* 15: 197–213.

Maslow, A. H. 1943. A theory of human motivation. *Psychological Review* 50, 370–396.

Roberts, Joan, E. 2001. Therapeutic effects of light in humans. In *Photobiology for the 21st Century*. ed. Thomas P. Coohill and Dennis P. Valenzeno, 17–29. Overland Park, KS: Valdenmar.

Chapter 4

Blount-Nuss, Gwenith, Kelly Leach Cate, and Heidi Lattimer. 2006. G.I. average Joe: The clothes do not make the man. *Journal of Articles in Support of the Null Hypothesis* 4(1): 9–16. www.jasnh.com/pdf/Vol4-No1-article2.pdf (accessed February 19, 2008).

Chechik, Jeremiah S. (Director) and John Hughes (Writer). 1898. *Christmas vacation* [Motion picture]. Burbank, CA: Warner Home Video.

Florida-Caribbean Cruise Association. (n.d.). Cruise industry overview—2007: State of the cruise industry. Pmbroke Pines, FL: Florida-Caribbean Cruise Association. www.f-cca.com/downloads/2007-overview.pdf (accessed March 20, 2008).

Genesis Class. n.d. www.worldcruise-network.com/projects/genesis/ (accessed June 6, 2008).

Henderson, Fred. 2005. The foundation of Carnival, October 1. www.shipsnostalgia.com/showthread.php?t=3004/ (accessed June 6, 2008).

Lempert, Phil, ed. 2004. Flu and cold season 2005: OTC remedies and the vaccine shortage. *Facts, Figures, & the Future*, December 13. www.factsfiguresfuture.com/archive/december_2004.htm.

Lincoln, Abraham. 1863. Abraham Lincoln online: Speeches and writings—The Gettysburg address. http://showcase.netins.net/web/creative/lincoln/speeches/gettysburg.htm (accessed March 15, 2008).

Mulford, M., J. Orbell, C. Shatto, and J. Stockard. 1998. Physical attractiveness, opportunity, and success in everyday exchange. *American Journal of Social Psychology*, *103* (6), 1565-1592.

The 100 oldest companies in the world. 2008, March 7. http://bizaims.com/Articles/Business+-+Economy/The+100+Oldest+Companies+in+the+World.html (accessed June 6, 2008).

Tarses, Mark. 1999. Tulipmania.com. www.sunwayco.com/tulipmania.html (accessed February 24, 2008).

The Tulip Mania. (n.d.). http://en.wikisource.org/wiki/The_Tulip_Mania (accessed February 24, 2008, originally published in *Harper's New Monthly Magazine,* April 1876).

Twain, Mark. 1869. *Innocents abroad.* Hartford, CT: American Publishing.

World Bank. 2005. *Income and poverty, 2005.* Washington DC: World Bank, United Nations Development Program.

Wright, Richard A. 1996. A brief history of the first 100 years of the automobile industry in the United States. In *After the muscle cars, the world comes to an end.*

Detroit, MI: Wayne State University, Department of Communications. www.theautochannel.com/mania/industry.orig/history/chap14.html (accessed March 5, 2008).

Chapter 5

Allen, James. 1902. *As a man thinketh*. New York.
Allport, G. W. 1935. Attitudes. In *Handbook of social psychology*, ed. C. Murchison, 798–844. Worcester, MA: Clark University Press.
Perloff, Richard M. 2003. *The dynamics of persuasion*. Mahwah, NJ: Lawrence Erlbaum.

Chapter 6

Adams, Noel. 2001. Why is GM crushing their EV1s? December 2. www.electrifyingtimes.com/ev1crush.html (accessed June 5, 2008).
Fields, W. C. (n.d.). Brainy quotes. www.brainyquote.com/quotes/authors/w/w_c_fields.html (accessed June 5, 2008).
Moore, Bill. 2003. Passion may save California's EVs. *EV World,* March 29. www.evworld.com/article.cfm?storyid=511 (accessed March 5, 2008).
U.S. Department of Education. 1999. EV America: 1999 General Motors EV1 w Ni/MH. Vehicle Specifications. http://avt.inel.gov/pdf/fsev/eva/ev1_eva.pdf (accessed March 5, 2008).
U.S. Government Accountability Office. 2006. Contractor's national evaluation did not find that the youth anti-drug media campaign was effective in reducing youth drug use. http://www.gao.gov/new.items/d06818.pdf (accessed March 3, 2008).
Wielage, Mark, and Rod Woodcock. 1988. The rise and fall of beta. *Videofax,* 5. www.geocities.com/videoholic2000/RiseandFall.htm (accessed March 20, 2008).

Chapter 7

American Marketing Association. 2003. *2003 e-mail rules, policies, and practices survey,* May 28. www.amanet.org/press/amanews/Email_Survey2003.htm (accessed June 8, 2008).

Aristotle. 1984. *The rhetoric and the poetics of Aristotle.* Book 2. Modern Library College ed. Trans. W. Rhys Roberts and Ingram Bywater. New York: McGraw-Hill, 92–120.

Berlyne, Daniel Ellis. 1960. *Conflict, arousal, and curiosity.* New York: McGraw-Hill.

BIGresearch. 2006. *Simultaneous media usage survey*, September 20. www.bigresearch.com (accessed June 8, 2008).

Bureau of Labor Statistics. 2007. American time use survey. *News: United States Department of Labor,* June 28.

Conway, Jack (Director). 1947. *The Hucksters.* 1947. Hollywood, CA: Metro-Goldwyn-Mayer.

Engineers' Perception of Electronic Distributors. 1991. *Electronic Engineering Times*, August 26.

Grow, Brian. 2005. The great rebate runaround. *BusinessWeek,* November 23. www.businessweek.com/bwdaily/dnflash/nov2005/nf20051123_4158_db016.htm.

Hauser, Gerard A. Aristotle's list of emotions. http://spot.colorado.edu/~hauserg/ArEmotList.htm (accessed March 12, 2008).

Knowledge@Emory. 2008. *The hidden influence of emotions on consumers' choices*, January 16. http://knowledge.emory.edu/article.cfm?articleid=1115#/.

Manley, Fred. 1999. Nine ways to improve an ad . . . to death. *Communication Arts*, March–April, 77–79.

Ortony, Andrew, and Terence J. Turner. 1990. What's basic about basic emotions? *Psychological Review* 97: 315–331. www.cs.northwestern.edu/~ortony/papers/basic%20emotions.pdf.

Parker, Ed. 1982. *Infinite insights into Kenpo: Vol. 1. Mental stimulation.* Los Angeles: Delsby Publications.

Toffler, Alvin. 1970. *Future shock.* New York: Random House.

Chapter 8

Campbell-Kelly, Martin, and Aspray, Willaim. 2004. *Computer: A history of the information machine.* 2nd ed. Boulder, CO: Westview Press.

IBM Archives, 1930s. (n.d.). www-03.ibm.com/ibm/history/history/decade_1930.html (accessed March 15, 2008).

NCR Corporation. (n.d.). Company profile, information, business description, history, background information on NCR Corporation. www.referenceforbusiness.com/history2/32/Ncr-Corporation.html (accessed March 15, 2008).

Primary Color. (n.d.). About us. www.primarycolor.com/about_us.php.

Chapter 9

The Energizer Bunny. (n.d.). http://adage.com/century/icon05.html (accessed March 24, 2008).

Frieswick, Kris. What's wrong with this picture? *CFO Magazine*, January 1, 2003. www.cfo.com/article.cfm/3007726/1/c_3046585 (accessed March 30, 2008).

O'Neill, Jerry. 2002. The new Polaroid: After chapter 11, October 1. www.imaginginfo.com/article/article.jsp?siteSection=27&id=818&pageNum=1/ (accessed March 30, 2008).

Polaroid. 2008. Notification of Polaroid Instant Film Availability. www.polaroid.com/ifilm/en/index.html (accessed March 30, 2008).

RosenblumTV. 2007. Polaroid and Darwin, September 25. http://rosenblumtv.wordpress.com/2007/09/25/polaroid-and-darwin/ (accessed March 30, 2008).

Index